CURIOUS COUNTRY
CUSTOMS

CURIOUS COUNTRY
CUSTOMS

JEREMY
HOBSON

David and Charles

For Grace; with love

A DAVID & CHARLES BOOK
Copyright © David & Charles Limited 2007

David & Charles is an F+W Publications Inc. company
4700 East Galbraith Road
Cincinnati, OH 45236

First published in the UK in 2007

Text copyright © Jeremy Hobson 2007
Illustrations copyright © David & Charles 2007
For photography © see p224

A catalogue record for this book is available from the British Library.

ISBN-13: 978-0-7153-2658-9
ISBN-10: 0-7153-2658-9

Printed in Finland by WS Bookwell
for David & Charles
Brunel House, Newton Abbot, Devon

Commissioning Editor: Mic Cady
Assistant Editor: Louise Clark
Copy Editor: Rebecca Snelling
Designer: Eleanor Stafford
Production Controller: Kelly Smith

Visit our website at www.davidandcharles.co.uk

David & Charles books are available from all good bookshops; alternatively you can contact our Orderline on 0870 9908222 or write to us at FREEPOST EX2 110, D&C Direct, Newton Abbot, TQ12 4ZZ (no stamp required UK only); US customers call 800-289-0963 and Canadian customers call 800-840-5220.

Contents

January

The New Year	11
New Year's Eve	12
Haxey Hood Game	14
Twelfth Night (Epiphany) Cake	17
Straw Bear Festival	18
Goathland Plough Stot	20
Blessing the Plough	22
Wassailing	23
Wassailing the Apple Tree	25
Dwile Flonking	26
Up-Helly-Aa	27

February

Candlemas	29
Rocking Ceremony	31
Hurling the Silver Ball	32
Blessing the Salmon Nets	33
Valentine's Day	34
Crochon Crewys	36
Olney Pancake Day Race	37
Shrove Tuesday and Lent	39
Scarborough Skipping Festival	41
Purbeck Marblers' and Stonecutters' Day	42
Shrovetide Football	43
29 February	46

March

Swearing on the Horns	47
Kiplingcotes Derby	48
Tichborne Dole	50
Lady Day	52
Easter Customs	53
Maundy Thursday	56
World Marbles Championships	58
Furmitty	59
Britannia Coconut Dancers	60
Dinas Bran Pilgrimage	61
Hare Pie Scramble and Bottle Kicking	62
World Coal Carrying Championships	64
Biddenden Dole	66

April

April Fools' Day	67
Passing the Penny	68
Tuttimen Hocktide Festival	69
St George and the Dragon	72
Shakespeare Procession	74
Letting the White Bread Meadow	76
Squab, Parsley and Licky Pies	78

May

May Day	79
Knutsford Royal May Day	81
'Obby 'Oss Ceremony	82
Sweeps' Festival	84
Cheese Rolling	85
Furry Dance	88
Planting the Penny Hedge	90
Blessing the Sea	92
Rogation Day and Beating the Bounds	93
Scorton Silver Arrow Tournament	95
Woolsack Race	96
Hunting of the Earl of Rone	97
Well Dressing	98
Garland Day	100

June

Duck Feast	101
West Linton Whipman Play	102
Nettle Eating Contest	103
Summer Solstice	104
Midsummer Cushions	105
The Green Man	106
Bawming the Thorn	107
Guid Nychburris	108
Hepworth Feast	109
Golowan Festival	110
Braw Lads' Gathering	111
Morris Dancing	113
Warcop Rush Bearing	115
Gâche Cake and Beanjar	116

July

Love Feast	117
Wenlock Olympian Games	118
Whalton Bale	118
Tynwald Ceremony	119
Kilburn Feast	120
Dunmow Flitch Trial	121
Eyemouth Herring Queen Festival	123
Sham Fight	124
Church Clipping	125
Ebernoe Horn Fair	127
Swan-Upping	128
Groaty Dick and Filbelly	130

August

Bonsall Hen Race	131
Puck Fair	133
The Burryman	136
Scarecrow Festival	138
Marhamchurch Revels	140
Rose of Tralee Festival	141
Rush-Cart Ceremony	142
Burning the Bartle	143
Bank and Public Holidays	145
Oul' Lammas Fair	147
Dulse and Yellowman	148

September

Crying the Neck	149
Braemar Gathering	151
Abbots Bromley Horn Dance	153
Egremont Crab Fair and Gurning Championships	156

Hop Hoodening 158
Widecombe Fair 159
Struan Micheil 160
Gathering St Michael's
    Carrots 161
Fairs 162

October

Weather Warnings 165
British Lawn Mower Racing
    Grand Prix 166
Old Man's Day 167
Lost in the Dark Bells 167
World Conker
    Championships 168
Moot Horn Curfew 170
Titchfield Carnival 172
Stow Gypsy Horse Fair 173
Oyster Feast 174
Halloween 176
Hop-Tu-Naa 178

November

Tar Barrel Racing 179
Turning the Devil's Stone 180
Bonfires 181
Wroth Silver Ceremony 183
Horseman's Word Ceremony 185
Armistice Day and
    Martinmas 187
Firing the Fenny Poppers 190
The Biggest Liar in the
    World Competition 191
Blessing the Silkies 192

St Edmund's Bun 193
The Court Leet 194
National Flowers of Britain 195
Atholl Brose 196

December

Christmas: Origins
    and Customs 197
Tin Can Band 199
Tom Bawcock's Eve 200
Star-Gazey Pie 201
Tolling the Devil's Knell 202
Blessing the Crib 202
Christmas Day Dip 203
Christmas Day Superstitions 204
Marshfield Paper Boys 205
Boxing Day
    (St Stephen's Day) 206
Mason's Walk 208
Holy Innocent's Day 209
Mari Lwyd Mummers' Play 210
Mumming Plays 212
Fire Festivals 214

Customs By Region 217

Index 222

INTRODUCTION

There must, one would suppose, be a logical reason why 13 men might sit in a pub on a June evening, all wearing hats adorned with duck feathers; or why virtually the entire population of two villages attempt to chase a ball across a 2-mile (3km) stretch of countryside; or several outwardly normal-looking sensible people career hysterically downhill after a rolling round of cheese?

What previous events inspire burly athletes to pick up a bag of coal, or a bale of wool, in order to compete against one another? And why, in the early hours of Easter Sunday, May Day or at the dawn of the summer Solstice do groups of solemn worshippers climb Welsh mountains; wash their faces in the early morning dew; and watch the arrival of the sun from the circle at Stonehenge?

Many happenings are specific to a certain area of Britain. The West Country, Scotland and Northern England, for example, have more than their fair share of curious customs that cannot be witnessed anywhere else in the country, whereas it seems that Wales and Ireland have more generalized traditions, superstitions and folklore, most of which are based around singing and dancing – surely the two most ancient methods of

warding off evil spirits and encouraging the favours of gods associated with hunting and crop fertility?

Although many customs undoubtedly have pagan origins, in some cases they have been 'adopted' by the Church in order to suit their own ends. Others were devised by countryside workers and everyday folk as a means of creating a time of reunion with family and friends, safe in the knowledge that there was no need to pick up a tool or harness a plough, and giving a legitimate excuse for the village to turn out, eat, drink and be merry – all the while knowing that tomorrow there was more work to be done and their small world would move into its next season. Yet other customs are not old at all but will no doubt become established traditions in future years. Old or new, all have one thing in common, that of a sense of belonging and a time for innocent fun – long may they continue and flourish.

Curious Country Customs should appeal to people passionate about Britain, readers interested in folklore and rural history, and to those who delight in finding a logical reason for everything, no matter how obscure! It also provides a database of dates, times, locations and opportunities for

those who wish to watch or even participate – as all the customs detailed are still in existence today.

The book focuses on individual events held at a specific place, but it is worth mentioning that a few, such as Up-Helly-Aa (see page 27), a fire-fest held at Lerwick, are also celebrated at around the same time in other areas of Scotland. Some customs and traditions described also move months from time to time, due either to links with the phases of the moon or, rather more mundanely, because a particular feast day falls mid-week and the organizers have decided that it would be better held on a weekend when a greater attendance can be expected. The biggest 'moveable feast' is Easter and for that reason it has its own chapter, which can be found between March and April.

Before considering attending any event, it is advisable to contact one of the nearest tourist offices in the region or to look on one of the many website links.

JEREMY HOBSON

THE NEW YEAR

Some 700 years before Julius Caesar came to power in 46BC, the Roman year comprised ten months and began on 25 March (Lady Day), a date that crops up regularly in country customs (see page 52).

The arrival of Caesar saw the creation of the Julian calendar and by the time Britain began using it there were 12 months of 30 days and a 13th of five. If it were to have continued, we would by now be about eight years behind ourselves and probably celebrating New Year's Day on 13 September as they do in Ethiopia, where the Julian calendar is still used.

In the late 1500s the Gregorian calendar, devised by Pope Gregory XIII, was introduced. This was implemented at different times throughout Britain, but for Wales and the majority of England it appears to have been in common usage by 1752. Scotland's changeover was earlier than this and in 1599 the Privy Council resolved that the following year should officially begin on 1 January.

Up in Arms

The new calendar was not popular and it caused a public outcry throughout Britain with people demanding that they should be given back their 'lost' days. This protest is still commemorated by the 200 inhabitants of Gwaun Valley near Fishguard, Dyfed, Wales, who belatedly welcome in the New Year on 13 January in a ceremony known as Hen Galan.

New Year's Eve

In Scotland, the eve of the New Year has traditionally been of supreme importance and still takes precedence over Christmas. Nowadays it is a time of fun and light-hearted tradition, but underneath the rejoicing is an element of superstition and ritual.

Up until the beginning of the 20th century it was common practice for Scottish people to go around houses and shops carrying dried cow-hides and chanting rhymes, which it was hoped would keep at bay fairies, evil spirits and hostile forces of every kind. At each home the hide was singed in the fire and members of the household were required to smell it as a charm against all things evil and harmful.

First Footing

Better known is the custom of First Footing, when, at midnight, armed with a bottle of whisky and gifts, people visit their neighbours in the hope of bringing them luck. In England it is still the custom for a dark-haired man to 'let in the New Year': the man leaves the house by the back door just before midnight on New Year's Eve and on the stroke of midnight knocks on the front door. The householder opens the door and traditionally receives from him the following gifts: salt for seasoning, silver for wealth, coal for warmth, a match for kindling and bread for sustenance.

THE WELSH WAY

In Wales, if the first visitor is a woman and a man opens the door bad luck will follow, as it will if a red-haired man is the first male to cross the threshold. Another New Year custom that used to be carried out throughout Wales was the giving of the Calennig – a token piece of fruit, usually an apple or an orange. From dawn until noon on 1 January, groups of young boys would visit all the homesteads in their locality carrying with them branches of evergreen and water drawn from the nearest well: they would then use the twigs to splash people with the water and in return be given the Calennig – the custom has all but died out and, were the local lads to try it today, they would no doubt receive a court order and an ASBO rather than any reward!

In Wales, if you pay off your debts on New Year's Day it is considered good luck. On the other hand, to do the same elsewhere in Britain is deemed bad luck.

Manx Ways

In the Isle of Man, New Year's Day used to be known as Laa Nolick beg, or 'little Christmas Day', and the first person or creature you met after leaving home decided whether or not you would have good fortune through the coming year; to meet either a splay-footed person or a cat, for example, was considered unfortunate. Great care also had to be taken when sweeping up around the Manx house on New Year's morning: the dust had to be swept so that it travelled from the door towards the hearth. If this wasn't done, the good fortune of the family would be swept from the home for that particular year.

Haxey Hood Game

Haxey, Lincolnshire (6 January, unless the 6th falls on a Sunday, in which case it is held on the 5th)

The pleasant village of Haxey goes mad on one day of the year as its youth and those from nearby Westwoodside battle it out on the fields and down the streets to get the Hood to their favourite pub.

Gone With the Wind

The traditional story behind the game is that in the 14th century Lady Mowbray, wife of a local landowner, was riding home from church when a high wind blew away her scarlet hood. No less than 13 labourers chased after it in the hope of retrieving it for her, but the one who actually captured the hood was apparently so shy that it was left to another of the group – who obviously had more experience of social situations – to hand it back to the lady. She named the pair Fool and Lord respectively and in reward for their gallantry bestowed the rent from a piece of land in the village, still known as Hoodlands, to finance an annual game in which 13 men dressed in scarlet competed for the prize of a hood. Since then, the game – which has been described as a kind of debased rugby football – has undergone many changes and is now nothing more than a free-for-all carried out between teams from the two villages.

Another possibility regarding the origins of the game is that it is connected with a pagan fertility festival. In Viking culture a bull was often sacrificed at this time of the year and its head (hood?) was used as a sort of football in the hope that its blood would ensure a good growing season. The wand used by the Lord Boggan (see right) might have represented the sword and blood associated with the animal's slaughter.

How to Play

Whatever its roots, the Haxey Hood Game is played with a piece of rope bound with leather, known as the Sway Hood, and takes place between members of the crowd who are overlooked by 13 referees (representing the 13 original labourers). One is appointed the Fool, who is allowed to kiss any lady he chooses, one the Lord and the remaining 11 are the Boggans (spelt variously as boggan, boggin or boggon), with one as the Chief Boggan. The ten ordinary Boggans wear fancy dress, including red jumpers, while the Chief Boggan wears a red hunting coat and the Fool sackcloth trousers and a patched jacket. The Lord wears a hunting jacket and a top hat and carries a wand of office made up of bound willow sticks (13 in all) with a red ribbon attached to the top.

Before the game begins at about 2.30pm, the Fool recites a speech from an old mounting block in front of the church known as the Mowbray Stone: in it he gives his instructions about rough play, avoiding damage and injuring others before giving the traditional cry of 'Hoose agen hoose, toon agen toon, if tha meets a man nok im doon, but doant 'ot im', which translates as 'House against house, town against town, if you meets a man, knock him down but don't hurt him'.

Smoking Ban

Presumably, the Fool was not a greatly sought-after job in years gone by, as, after the speech had been read and prior to the days of Health and Safety or risk assessments, the strips of paper that had been used to decorate his costume were set alight – an amiable custom known as Smoking the Fool. Today the Fool is in less danger as he is symbolically smoked by damp straw set alight behind the Mowbray Stone.

About an hour after the speech the Lord leads the participants to Upperthorpe Hill where the game is to begin. Before he does, 12 other 'hoods' constructed from pieces of sacking and tied with red ribbon are thrown into the air. The youngsters in the crowd run for them and anyone who manages to catch one and get it past the line of Boggans is given a small financial reward.

Once the game has begun it can last for as long as three or four hours, the object being to get the Sway Hood to one or other of the public houses located in Haxey or Westwoodside where, after being anointed with beer, it remains on display for the forthcoming year.

The symbolic smoking of the Fool during the Haxey Hood Game

TWELFTH NIGHT (EPIPHANY) CAKE

Twelfth Night, 5 January, marks the end of the Christmas period. In Britain it was usual to make a simple fruit cake to be eaten at this time and superstition dictated that it should contain some good luck charms or 'favours' such as cloves, twigs or even a piece of rag. The most common addition to the cake mix though was a bean and a pea, one being placed in each half. As the visitors arrived, ladies were served from the left-hand 'pea' side, men from the right. Whoever got the bean was 'king' for the night and the recipient of the pea, the 'queen', and for the rest of the evening the pair ruled supreme whatever their position in daily life.

Whoever found the bean in their piece of cake was also considered to be a sort of guardian angel for their family for the forthcoming year, so it was often arranged that a senior family member would receive the 'gift'.

French Tradition

Despite the disappearance of the Twelfth Night, or Epiphany, cake in Britain, it is still an important part of the Christmas/New Year tradition elsewhere in Europe, especially in France where the *gateaux* or *galette des Rois* is found in every village bakery. Nowadays a small pottery figure takes the place of the bean and each cake is supplied with a gold paper crown.

Straw Bear Festival

Straw Bear Tuesday follows Plough Monday and is commemorated in the Cambridgeshire Fens at Whittlesea (sometimes spelt Whittlesey), where a local farmer is persuaded to dress up in a costume of straw fashioned loosely into the shape of a bear. In the past, the person chosen to be the bear had great lengths of tightly woven straw bands wound around his arms, legs and body. Two sticks were then fastened to his shoulders, the points of which met as a triangle over his head: more straw was then twisted around these until a cone effect was achieved. (Not just any old straw would do though: at harvest time the best available was selected and stored until the following January.) A strong chain or rope was then fastened under the 'bear's' armpits before he was taken to dance in front of the village houses, in return for which he and his handler would receive gifts of money or food and drink.

Despite the similarity the festival has with the cruel practice of training live bears to dance at fairs, it is unlikely that there is any direct connection: it is more likely the custom stems from the tradition of using straw effigies throughout Britain and Europe to celebrate our ties with and dependence on the land, our closeness with nature and the mystery of the seasons.

In Disguise

Molly dancers, in common with other troupes, perform with blackened faces. The participants were often illiterate farm workers who needed the confidence of a 'guise' (disguise) so they would not be made fun of by their non-performing peers. In addition, the dancers and performers could perform mischievous acts – often involving extracting money from the populace and their employers – so they were keen to keep their identities secret for fear of the consequences at some later date.

Successful Revival

In the early 20th century the straw bear tradition lost favour with the authorities, who considered it to be nothing more than an exercise in begging, but it was revived at Whittlesea in the 1980s and evolved into the highly popular Straw Bear Festival of today that features concerts, dances and a procession around the town. Linking the event once again to Plough Monday, the procession now incorporates a plough. As part of these festivities, lumbering men wearing farmers' hats, wreaths of evergreen foliage and hob-nailed boots carry out Molly dancing (a type of Morris dancing peculiar to the fenlands of East Anglia).

The 'bear' in his straw costume makes his way to the festival, curiously here by bicycle

Goathland Plough Stot

The first Monday after Twelfth Day (6 January) is traditionally known as Plough Monday, marking the end of the Christmas period for the agricultural community. In British folklore the plough was more than just a tool: it was a symbol of power and productivity and on Plough Monday the working men would carry a plough around the village, taking the opportunity to enjoy themselves before the start of a long, arduous year. At Goathland, part of these festivities involved joining a team of long-sword dancers who would dance around the village begging for alms and threatening to plough a furrow through the garden of anyone who refused to contribute!

The long-sword dancers of Goathland Plough Slot

Dancing …

There are still several long-sword dance teams around the county of Yorkshire, but Goathland's is one of the oldest – the Plough Stots have been around for at least 150 years. The dance weaves its way through the village streets and consists of a number of intricate moves, the essence of which involves each dancer holding the tip of his neigh-bour's sword as they circle and twist through the patterns. At the end, all the swords should become entwined in what is known as a 'lock' and this is often lowered over the head of one of the comic characters who accompany the dancers: Betty, dressed in rags and shawl; T' Awd Man with his odd stockings and felt hat, the Gentleman, the Fool, Old Issac and several more. Some of the dancers wear tunics of pink and blue over grey trousers: the tunic colours are political and represent either the Tory or Whig party, while the trousers are reminders of the uniform of those soldiers who fought in the Crimean War.

> ### Long-Sword Dance
> The long-sword dance is peculiar to Yorkshire: the earliest record dates back to 1789 but the widespread distribution of the dance suggests that it may be much older. Long-sword is a dignified dance, sometimes militaristic in its performance. The old, now extinct rigid sword dance from the Tyne Valley, first recorded in 1715, was probably very similar to the modern long-sword dance.

… and Feasting

The day's festivities begin at around 9.30am and culminate with the Stot Rosh – a huge roast dinner followed by speeches and awards to those members who have deserved recognition over the preceding year – and a barn dance to which all are welcome.

As a concession to modern-day working schedules, the Plough Stot and Sword Dance now take place on the Saturday following the traditional Plough Monday.

BLESSING THE PLOUGH

Blessing the Plough services are held at many churches on Plough Sunday, the first Sunday after Twelfth Day (6 January). Some of the best known take place at Chichester and Exeter cathedrals, Sherborne Abbey in Dorset and Hedenham Church in Norfolk.

The origins of Plough Sunday go at least as far back as medieval times when, on the first Sunday after Epiphany (which marked the end of the Christmas holidays and the subsequent return to work for all agricultural workers), the parish ploughs, bedecked with ribbons, would be dragged to church to be blessed. Nowadays a single symbolic plough is used in the service, which is still intended as a service of prayer and blessing for all those involved in agriculture.

The service in all churches follows pretty much the same format, part of which involves the following words, recited by the minister:

"God speed the plough and the ploughman, the farm and the farmer/God speed the plough, on hillside and in valley; on land which is rich, and on land which is poor; in countries beyond our seas, and in our homeland/God speed the plough, in fair weather and in foul, in success and disappointment, in rain and in wind, in frost and sunshine."

To this the congregation respond: 'God speed the plough.' This is a wish for success and prosperity, originating from a 15th-century song, sung by ploughmen as they customarily went from door to door soliciting 'plough money' on Plough Monday.

WASSAILING

The word wassail is thought derive from the Saxon greeting 'waes hael', meaning 'be well' or 'be hale and hearty'. At the beginning of each year the lord of the manor would shout 'waes hael' and his assembled minions were expected to reply with the words 'drink hael', meaning 'drink and be healthy'. Through the ages, wassailing has come to mean the practice of festive merrymaking and the toasting of good health and encouraging good fortune in the coming year with a wassail drink. Objects such as apple trees were also wassailed to encourage bountiful crops (see page 25).

Some wassailing songs became part of the Christmas festivities and, like the carol singers of today, the original wassailers expected drink, money, Christmas food (preferably all three) in return for their offer of good wishes and luck for the year to come. On occasions, the singers could be quite blatant in their requests: 'So give us some Figgy Pudding ... we won't go until we've got some' is a refrain that is still well known. The practice of going from door to door carrying a wassail bowl did not begin until the 15th century.

The Wassail Drink

The traditional ingredients of wassail were ale or rough cider seasoned with spices and honey, but there were also regional variations, probably the most common of which was 'lambswool'. This contained ale, baked apples, sugar, spices, eggs and cream served with little pieces of bread. Opinions differ as to the origin of the name, some believing that it came from the bread's similarity to a lamb's fleece as it floated on the top of the drink, while others think that it is a derivation of the Irish apple-gathering festival La mas ubhal.

APPLES, BEES AND CATTLE

It was not just apple trees that enjoyed the attentions of the wassailers: bee skeps or hives were wassailed in the hope that they would produce a huge crop of honey in the coming year, as were cattle. In some regions a special 'cow cake' was attached to the bull. The animal was then prodded and poked to make him toss his head and throw the cake – if it was tossed forwards, it was a good omen for the forthcoming year, but if it fell backwards, a poor harvest was forecast.

Wassailing the Apple Tree

Carhampton, Somerset (17 January)

The Butcher's Arms in Carhampton had kept the custom of Wassailing the Apple Tree (see page 23) alive in the village for years, so when it appeared that the piece of ground on which the old apple tree stood might be sold into less sympathetic hands, the then owners of the pub bought the land, thus ensuring a secure future for both the tree and tradition. Apple farming has long been an important part of the local economy in Somerset and in some areas apple cider formed part of a farm labourer's wage.

Anointing the Tree

In Carhampton, onlookers and participants begin arriving at sunset although the ceremony doesn't usually start until around 7.30pm, when the proceedings commence with the lighting of a bonfire.

Mulled cider and toasted bread is then brought out and the wassailing song is normally sung, or chanted, as a blessing, either as or just before the cider is sprinkled over the tree's roots. Carhampton has its own particular version of the song.

It might not have much merit in the eyes of the modern-day professional songwriter, but as the last three lines are repeated and the whole crowd join in, the noise created must surely go some way towards scaring off the demons!

The toast is then dipped into the cider bucket and placed in the branches of the tree in order to attract the good spirits – which apparently appear in the guise of robins the following morning – before folk songs are sung, guns fired into the air and drinks offered to the onlookers.

Dwile Flonking

Not until the 1960s did Dwile Flonking become a recognized 'sport'. Originally played outside The Farmer's Boy public house at Kensworth (why do so many of these midwinter customs involve licensed premises?) on 22 January, Dwile Flonking is now also played in the two Suffolk towns of Bungay and Beccles, where it is considered a summer rather than winter event. Nevertheless, the current owners of The Farmer's Boy are seriously considering reviving the competition again.

A Load of Drivel

Officially, the game is played by two teams of 12 players, but numbers can be flexible. First, a sugar beet is tossed to decide which team is going to 'flonk' first. Next the fielding team gathers in a circle, called a 'girter', enclosing a member of the other team, the 'flonker'. He holds a broom handle, usually known as the 'driveller', on top of which is a beer-soaked rag, the 'dwile' (an old Suffolk term for a dishcloth). At a signal, the girter dances around the flonker in a circle. He must flonk the dwile with the driveller so that it hits a girter team member.

> **What to Wear**
> *Authentic costume is encouraged among the players and the suggested dress code consists of a 'pork-pie' hat, a collarless shirt or yeoman's smock, 'lijahs' (trousers tied at the knees with baler twine) and hobnailed boots — with a clay pipe stuck in the mouth.*

His score depends on which part of the body he hits: the usual scoring is three points for a hit on the head, two for the body and one for the legs. If, after two shots, the flonker hasn't scored, he is 'swadged' and has to drink beer from a chamber pot within a specified time.

Up-Helly-Aa

Lerwick, Scotland (last Tuesday in January)

During Britain's biggest fire festival and torchlight procession, over 900 colourfully dressed guisers follow the Guizer Jarl's (an elected chief of proceedings, who used to be known as the Worthy Chief Guiser) army of Vikings and their longship through the darkened streets of the town before 800 flaming torches are thrown ceremonially into the boat.

The festival originally marked old Christmas Eve but from 1870 the celebrations were postponed until the end of January so as to commemorate the end of the winter festival of Yule, nowadays Christianized as the Christmas season. From its inception, the event at Lerwick has always been a lively affair – in 1824 a visiting Methodist missionary wrote in his diary that:

"The whole town was in an uproar: from twelve o clock last night until late this night, there was the blowing of horns, beating of drums, tinkling of old tin kettles, firing of guns, shouting, bawling, fiddling, fifeing, drinking and fighting. This was the state of the town all the night – the street was thronged with people … "

Bigger and Better

As Lerwick grew in size the celebrations became more elaborate until it became customary to see burning tar barrels being dragged about the narrow streets or set alight at the harbour, with bands of rival tar-barrellers fighting anywhere and everywhere.

Midwinter Blues

Bygone revellers knew the importance of midwinter festivals as the short, dark days would have seen communities at their lowest ebb. Gatherings such as Up-Helly-Aa (meaning 'end of the holy days') would have been important dates in the calendar, as they provided a feel-good factor for the community.

Over time the festival became a more organized affair and the Viking theme, together with a torchlight procession, was introduced. However it was not until the late 1880s that a longship appeared and 1906 before a Guizer Jarl joined the proceedings. Nowadays, the procession to the harbour is accompanied by more tuneful music than that experienced by the 19th-century Methodist missionary but, although the official part of the evening ends when the torches are thrown into the mock Viking ship once it is floating in the water of the harbour, it is doubtful that he would have found it any the less noisy. After the burning of the longship, rockets are fired and the night of revelry continues with dancing and drinking in each of the town's dozen or more local halls.

There is also an Up-Helly-Aa festival at Scalloway, Shetland, which falls 11 days before the event at Lerwick.

A Viking aboard the longship at the Up-Helly-Aa

CANDLEMAS

According to the Church calendar, Candlemas (2 February) is the day for observing the ritual purification of Mary 40 days after the birth of Jesus and the presentation of Jesus to the Temple of Jerusalem: in fact, this was a Christian adaptation of a pagan practice acknowledging the fact that winter was halfway through.

The date's significance in country lore is that it lies midway between the winter solstice and the spring equinox, thus marking the point at which winter is half over. It resulted in a well-known rhyme saying that, 'A farmer should, on Candlemas Day, have half his corn and half his hay,' which meant that anyone having less than half their fodder left at this time could expect to experience problems later if the winter happened to be a particularly harsh one.

Groundhog Day

In America, 2 February is known as Groundhog Day. Folklore has it that if a groundhog emerges from its burrow on this day and fails to see its shadow because the weather is cloudy, winter will soon end. Conversely, if the groundhog does see its shadow because the weather is bright and clear, the creature will be frightened and run back into its hole and the winter will continue for six more weeks.

Superstitions

On Dartmoor, it was considered important to have removed all signs of greenery that had been hung up over the Christmas period by 2 February, as not to do so was tantamount to inviting death into the house during the coming year. And if you were to hear the sound of church bells on this date, they would indicate the death of a close friend or relation. Placing candles in every window of the house would, on the other hand, attract good luck. Altar candles were also consecrated at this time and smaller candles distributed after a church service on this day were taken home in the belief that they contained curative and protective powers.

Customs

There was a Scottish Candlemas custom whereby children would bring money to buy candles for the schoolroom. Later this developed into gifts for the schoolmaster himself – the boy giving the largest gift being appointed Candlemas King: it makes the bribe of 'an apple for the teacher' seem quite tame, especially when one considers that the Candlemas King's reign lasted for six weeks and it gained him a great many privileges, including that of being able to remit punishments!

Known as Olmbolc (or Imbolc) in the Celtic calendar, meaning either 'in the belly' or 'ewe's milk', Candlemas was celebrated by rituals that were intended to harness divine energy and ensure a steady supply of food until harvest-time some six months hence. Like many Celtic customs, the Olmbolc festivals centred on the lighting of fires, and Brigid, the pagan goddess of fire, healing and fertility, is celebrated at this time.

Rocking Ceremony

Blidworth, Nottinghamshire (Sunday closest to Candlemas)

This particular religious ceremony would appear to be unique to the Church of St Mary in the village of Blidworth. The origins go back at least 400 hundred years to a service known as the Presentation of the Temple, which is connected to Candlemas (see page 29). Banned in the Reformation, the custom has lapsed at least twice in the intervening time, but was fortunately revived: once after an absence of 150 years in 1842 and again in 1922.

The male child born in Blidworth parish nearest to Christmas Day is, as part of the tradition, rocked in an ancient, flower-bedecked cradle. After the ceremony the child receives a bible for use in later life and is then carried through the streets of the village. A local recitation accompanies the modern-day service.

Hurling the Silver Ball

St Ives, Cornwall (first Monday after 3 February)

There was a time when Hurling the Silver Ball was part of the tradition of many Cornish villages; nowadays only two – St Ives and St Columb – continue the practice. Of the two, the hurling at St Ives is a much more staid affair and is as unlike the event at St Columb held later in the year as it's possible to get. At the latter event, things get so boisterous that the shopkeepers barricade their windows and doors in preparation for the start of the scrum at 4.30pm. The battle between town and country then continues until 8pm, when a winner is declared.

A local pub sign commemorates the game

A Game of Catch

The custom at St Ives is nominally connected with the Feast of St Ia (or Eia), who fled from persecution in Ireland, miraculously crossed the Irish Sea on a leaf, gave St Ives its name and converted that part of Cornwall to Christianity.

On Feast Monday, the first Monday after 3 February, the St Ives game, formally contested between a team of those named Tom, Will or John on one side and all those with different Christian names on the other, is now more usually played between local schoolchildren. Proceedings begin at 9.30am with the blessing of the silver ball (which is not in fact silver at all but made from either apple-wood or cork and thinly coated with silver) at the holy well of St Ia at Porthmeor before the game commences an hour later at 10.30am.

Standing on the wall of the churchyard, the mayor throws the ball into the assembled crowd and it is passed from hand to hand through the streets and along the beach. Whoever is in possession of the ball when the clock strikes noon takes it back to the mayor who is waiting at the Guildhall to award the traditional 'crown' (25p) prize money.

Neighbourly Competition
Many years ago, the neighbouring village of Lelant, situated some 3 miles (5km) from St Ives, held its Feast Day on 2 February and it was the custom for the two places to compete against one another by placing goals similar to basketball nets at their respective parish churches. The game was altered to its present form when the population of St Ives outnumbered Lelant.

Blessing the Salmon Nets

Norham-on-Tweed, Northumberland (14 February)

On 14 February, just before midnight, the ancient ceremony of Blessing the Salmon Nets is performed at the Pool of Pedwell, where the glebe land of the vicar of Norham runs down to the river. This is an old salmon-fishing centre and the service is traditionally held in the last few moments before the new fishing season opens on 15 February. Everyone present repeats the ancient Pedwell prayer (a local blessing dedicated to the safety of fishermen and successful catches) and the boats put out promptly at midnight. If the first nets to be 'shot' bring in a salmon, the catch is presented to the vicar. The congregation at this service needn't worry too much about wearing Sunday Best and is instead advised to wrap up warmly, wear Wellington boots and carry torches.

The vicar of Norham blesses the salmon nets

VALENTINE'S DAY (14 FEBRUARY)

This is the day for lovers and birds. Nowadays we choose our Valentines and send them unsigned cards, but in years gone by men and women would put their names on slips of paper and draw lots as to who would be their 'lover' – sounds the sort of party to which invites would be in great demand! A more genteel way of finding a future husband or wife was to place some bay leaves under your pillow before retiring for the night and you would be sure to dream of your future partner.

What bird you saw on the morning of Valentine's Day was supposed to foretell the type of person you would marry: if a woman saw a robin flying overhead, it meant that she would marry a sailor. If she saw a sparrow, she would marry a poor man and be very happy; but best of all, if she saw a goldfinch, she would marry a millionaire. Birds themselves were also believed to choose their mates on 14 February.

RITUALS AND ROMANCE

Of the many rituals associated with Valentine's Day, a few are specific to certain areas. In Norfolk, Jack Valentine, otherwise known as Old Father Valentine or even Old

Love Tokens

In Wales, wooden love spoons were carved and given as gifts. Hearts, keys and keyholes were favourite decorations, meant to imply that the recipient could unlock the giver's heart.

Mother Valentine, is supposed to disappear into thin air after knocking at doors and leaving a present, while girls in Derbyshire would pray that their boyfriend called, otherwise they would suffer the humiliation of being deemed 'dusty' by her family and friends who then had to clean her with a broom or wisp of straw.

Apples seemed to play quite an important part in choosing a partner and predicting how many children the union was likely to produce. One tradition was if you recited the names of five or six possible suitors as the stem of an apple was twisted, the name being spoken as the stem snaps belonged to the person you would eventually marry. Cut an apple in half and count how many seeds are inside to discover the number of children you will have.

By the early 19th century Valentine's Day had become the excuse rather than the reason for a little legitimate begging and children bedecked with ribbons paraded the neighbourhood chanting such lines as:

"*Good morrow, Valentine.*
Please to give me a Valentine
And I'll be yours and you'll be mine ..."

An alternative rendition contains the following lines:

"*Good morrow, Valentine,*
God bless the baker,
You'll be the giver,
And I'll be the taker ..."

St Valentine

There seems to be no connection between Valentine, priest and martyr, beheaded in 269AD, and the practice of exchanging lover's greetings. In fact many of the traditions associated with the date stem from well before the saint's birth and unfortunate early demise.

CROCHON CREWYS

In the days before takeaways, it appears that the only way Welsh youths could get a good meal out at night was to perform the ritual of the Crochon Crewys, or the Lentern Crock. Unfortunately for them this opportunity was restricted to the eve of Shrove Tuesday (see page 37), and also involved a little work before any sustenance was forthcoming.

As soon as darkness set in, a number of youths would visit a house, generally a farm in the locality, and secretly place on the kitchen windowsill either a small pottery crock or a scooped-out turnip containing little bits of bread, salt, leek, cabbage or some other vegetable before then shouting out a rhyme or doggerel and running off. If all went according to plan, the kitchen door would be opened and members of the household would dash after the youthful visitors. Should one be caught, he or she was duty-bound to clean and shine all the boots in the house. Once the chore was completed, the youngster would be rewarded with a generous feast of pancakes. The custom continued to be popular right up until World War II.

Silk Finish

For some reason, the origins of which have seemingly been lost over the years, it was apparently essential that, after careful polishing, the boots cleaned by the person who was caught had to be given a vigorous wiping over with a silk handkerchief.

Olney Pancake Day Race

Olney, Buckinghamshire (Shrove Tuesday)

Most of today's pancake races have a short history, but there is evidence that those at Olney have been run since 1445. Here, competitors must be over 18 years of age, wear skirts and aprons, have their heads covered and have lived in the town for a certain period. Before the age of political correctness only true 'housewives' could compete, but nowadays it is possible to stretch the rules.

The race ends at the parish church, where the winner is kissed by a member of the clergy, and is followed by the shriving service, during which the competitors' frying pans are arranged around the font.

Ready, Steady, Go

At exactly five minutes to noon the women take their places at the starting line in the Market Place, then, at the sound of the Pancake Bell, they toss their homemade pancakes and take off in the direction of the church gate. The starter of the race wears a resplendent, if somewhat historically inaccurate, mixture of a plumed helmet reminiscent of those worn in the Napoleonic Wars and a red tunic as worn at the Battle of Waterloo. Whoever reaches the finishing line first can claim a 'kiss of peace' from the verger and a prayer book. She also receives a number of gifts from local shops and businesses. In recent years these have included the Liberal prize, the result of an alliance between Olney and the town of Liberal in Kansas, America.

> ### How the Race Began
> In 1445 an Olney housewife, engrossed in making her pancakes in the lead-up to Lent, made herself late for the shriving service. On hearing the bells summoning all parishioners to church, the poor woman panicked and dashed out of the house, pan and pancake in hand, still sporting her apron and mop cap.

Even Stevens

Since 1950 Liberal, which has always celebrated Shrove Tuesday with enthusiasm, decided to take a leaf out of Olney's book and stage their own race over the same distance (still traditionally measured at 415yds/381m). The two towns compare timings and awards are made accordingly. In 2007, Jane Hughes won Olney's contest in 73.5 seconds, but overall, Liberal were the winners of the transatlantic competition, taking their total wins over the year to 32, compared to Olney's 25.

Pancake racers sprint for the finish at Olney

SHROVE TUESDAY
AND LENT

Shrove Tuesday, the day when Christians traditionally confessed and were shriven of their sins before the solemn fast of Lent, has always been a tame affair in Britain (with nothing but pancakes, skipping and football) compared to the lavish carnivals and Mardi Gras festivals that take place in other countries.

The three days preceding Ash Wednesday (the first day of Lent) are traditionally known as Shrovetide, culminating in Shrove Tuesday, or Pancake Day. The usual explanation as to why pancakes were eaten on this day is that it was a means of using up rich ingredients such as milk and eggs before Lenten fasting began, but there is actually more significance to the dish than that. The recipe deliberately includes eggs to signify creation, flour as the 'staff of life,' salt for wholesomeness and milk for purity. Eating pancakes on Shrove Tuesday meant you wouldn't go without food in the forthcoming year, although to ensure this you had to eat them before 8pm.

JACK O'LENT

In Elizabethan times a scarecrow or puppet figure known by the name of Jack O'Lent was set up in many public places at the start of Lent so people had someone to blame for the lack of food during the forthcoming weeks. Thought to be based on either a pagan winter god or Judas, the effigy would be carried through the town before being burnt on a funeral pyre. Several public houses carrying the same name are still in existence today, particularly in the West Country.

LENT

The religious aspect of Lent is well known, and for many Christians it is a preparation for Easter, culminating in a feast of seasonal and symbolic foods. In the late 17th century girls in service took a rich fruit cake to their mothers on the fourth Sunday in Lent. Known as Simnel cake, it was decorated with 11 marzipan balls (representing the 12 Apostles, minus Judas Iscariot, the betrayer of Jesus). This custom eventually developed into Mothering Sunday and it became a tradition for all children to give their mothers posies of wild flowers such as daffodils and primroses.

The colour purple is linked with Lent for two reasons: one is its associations with mourning, reminding the believer of Jesus's death, the second being that it is a 'royal' colour and so celebrates Christ's coming as a king.

Because of its links with abstinence, it was considered inappropriate for couples to marry during Lent. This fact gave rise to the adage 'Marry in Lent, live to repent.'

Clean Sweep

The word 'shrove' is derived from 'shrive,' meaning 'confession through penance'. Lent is a time for cleaning in preparation for Easter and spring: first the soul is cleansed, then the kitchen and finally the rest of the house. Houses were lime-washed prior to or during Lent and in this way everything was made ready to face the season of Salvation and Rebirth. The tradition of 'spring-cleaning' stems from this religious observance.

Scarborough Skipping Festival

Scarborough, North Yorkshire (Shrove Tuesday)

As long ago as 1853 townspeople gathered on Shrove Tuesday on the South Foreshore at Scarborough to celebrate what was known as Ball Day. As a public holiday, it was one of the few days when apprentices and servants could be sure of having at least half a day to enjoy themselves. Along the sea front stalls offered all manner of edible and frivolous produce that was eagerly snapped up by people in holiday mood. A contemporary account relates that: 'Baskets and balls of various qualities and colours were prominent too and battledores [a type of racquet] and shuttlecocks were bought even by men and women. On this day, grown-up folks can skip and play without being thought childish.'

By 1903 it was recorded that, 'a few bairns were skipping near the lifeboat', and in 1927 a national publicity campaign declared the event to be the Scarborough Skipping Festival, which continues today.

Originally rung at noon on Shrove Tuesday as a signal for the housewives to begin making pancakes, the main purpose of the Pancake Bell today is to summon the thousands of skipping enthusiasts on to the foreshore in readiness for some frenzied exercise over long ropes.

Energy and Fertility
Several springtime activities associated with country customs have a link to Britain's Celtic past and make more sense if viewed as magical fertility rites performed to raise energy. The contests that take place in traditions such as Shrovetide skipping and football, for example, involve rough games between the sexes that, according to pagan thinking, stir up and increase the energies of the whole universe. A football is thought to symbolize the sun, which has to be conquered to secure a bountiful harvest.

Purbeck Marblers' and Stonecutters' Day

At noon on Shrove Tuesday the Freemen of the Ancient Order of Purbeck Marblers and Stonecutters are summoned to their annual meeting by the church bell of King Edward the Martyr in the town of Corfe Castle. It was traditionally expected that any apprentices wishing to join the Order must attend the meeting and submit their credentials – together with a quart of ale, a loaf of bread and, for some obscure reason, the sum of 33 pence. Bizarrely, the most recently married Freeman must bring a football with him, which, after the formalities of the gathering are brought to a close, is used in the traditional match played in the streets.

The 'pitch' is much shorter than when the game was played along the right-of-way running between the town and Poole Harbour, some 3 miles (5km) away – an important thoroughfare for the transportation of Purbeck marble on its journey from the quarry to the boats waiting to ship it all over the country.

Shrovetide Football

Alnwick, Northumberland; Ashbourne, Derbyshire; Jedburgh, Borders

The practice of playing football at Shrovetide is a popular one and it is generally conceded that association football developed from it. Three traditional, volatile and energetic games still take place at Alnwick, Ashbourne and Jedburgh.

Shrovetide football is still played in several locations

Alnwick Shrovetide Football (Northumberland)

Two teams each comprising anything between 100 to 150 players represent the parishes of St Michael and St Paul. The game was first recorded here in 1762 and played in the streets until 1827, when the then Duke of Northumberland, whose ancestral home is Alnwick Castle, provided a field at the North Peth. In later years the Shrove Tuesday game moved to the Pastures. The length of pitch here is unusual as it measures one furlong (approximately 436yds/400m). The goalposts themselves are worth a mention too; decorated with lots of greenery, they measure 4ft 7in (1.5m).

Kick-off is at 2pm after the ball has been carried from the castle in a procession led by a piper playing the bagpipes. After the game and presentations, the ball becomes the property of whoever manages to get it out of the Pastures: there is plenty of competition to retain the ball as a memento and it is not unknown for the most determined would-be owner to resort to swimming the river!

Ashbourne Ball Game (Derbyshire)

The Ashbourne Shrove Tuesday ball game is one of the most famous still being played, although there are undoubtedly others that can claim a longer history. Taking place between the Up'ards and Down'ards, it starts at 2pm, when a specially prepared ball – slightly larger than a football and filled with cork – is thrown in by a visiting guest of honour. The goals are two mills situated some 3 miles (5km) apart, and the ball may be kicked, carried or thrown. Often the ball is fought for in the stream that runs through the 'pitch' and the game may last for several hours, sometimes finishing well after dark. If there's no score, the game will usually be resumed the following day.

Jedburgh Hand Ba' Game (Roxburghshire)

This is also known as the Fasteneen, or Fastern's E'en Ba' Game, on account of the fact that it traditionally takes place on Fastern's E'en, an alternative name for Shrove Tuesday. In Jedburgh, however, locals insist that Fastern's E'en is actually the first Tuesday after the first new moon after Candlemas. As this almost always coincides with Shrove Tuesday, they could perhaps be laying themselves open to accusations of nit-picking!

Either way, the Jedburgh Hand Ba' Game begins at Mercat Cross and starts with the throwing of the ball into the crowd. It is a contest between the Guppies and the Downs, that is between those born either north or south of an imaginary line running through the base of the cross: south is Up and north is Down. Guppies score, or 'hail', by throwing a ball over the castle wall; Downs by rolling the ball into an underground stream. There are no rules, which is just as well as there is no referee.

By 1704 it was reckoned that the game had become so violent that the burgh elders were forced to put a stop to it: reluctant to have their traditions taken away from them, the townsfolk overcame the edict by developing much smaller balls made of straw-stuffed leather and decorated with ribbons. Even so, a second attempt to stop the newer, slightly gentler game was made in 1848, but that too was overruled due to public pressure.

Heads you Lose

There is a school of thought that believes when the tradition first started, it was played with the severed heads of English raiders!

29 February

The tradition of a woman asking a man to marry her on 29 February is believed to have begun in 5th-century Ireland when St Bridget complained to St Patrick about the fact that only men had the right to propose marriage to their loved ones. Being a bit of a 'new man' in his thinking, the generous Patrick decreed that any yearning, lovelorn female should have her turn on this one day. It was reasoned that, since this extra day every four years existed only to rectify a problem in the calendar, it might as well also be used to put right this inequality between men and women.

The first documentation of this practice dates back to 1288, when Scotland actually passed a law legally permitting women to make the first move. At the same time it was also made law that any man who declined such a proposal must pay a fine, which could range from a kiss to the giving of a silk dress or a pair of gloves. The rejected woman could only accept the gift if, as it was handed over, she could prove that she was wearing a scarlet petticoat. According to English law, however, this day was best ignored and such frivolous shenanigans therefore had no legal status south of the border.

Swearing on the Horns

Highgate area of London (twice-yearly in March and July)

Not strictly a 'country' custom due to its location, this is nevertheless an interesting one. It dates back to 1635 when many of Highgate's inns made any stranger to the area swear a humorous oath on a pair of antlers. The custom may have originated among graziers, who halted on their way to the meat market at Smithfield. After completing the oath, the visitor was granted the Freedom of Highgate and had the right to kiss the most beautiful girl in the room. The ceremony was a riotous occasion described by Lord Byron as consisting of 'dance and draught till morn'.

Times change though and this venerable custom is nowadays performed at only a few local hostelries such as The Wrestlers, The Red Lion and Sun, and The Flask.

In case you fancy going in search of bread, beer and a beautiful blonde though, you might like to practice the oath:

" I Swear, by the Rules of sound Judgment
that I will not eat Brown Bread when I can have White,
except I like the Brown better;
that I will not Drink Small Beer when I can get Strong,
except I like the small Beer better;
But I will kiss the Maid in preference to the Mistress,
if I like the Maid better;
but sooner than lose a good chance
I will kiss them both.
So Help Me, Billy Bodkin. "

Kiplingcotes Derby

Supposedly the oldest flat race in England, the Kiplingcotes Derby dates back to 1519. The rules, drawn up in 1618, stated that:

> "*A horse race to be observed and ridd yearly on the third Thursday in March; open to horses of all ages, to convey horsemen's weight, ten stones, exclusive of saddle, to enter ye post before eleven o'clock on the morning of ye race. The race to be run before two.*"

In other words, no one knows just how many horses are likely to enter until the morning of the race itself; anyone racing under the weight of 10 stone (64kg) (and the race nowadays includes women) must carry lead weights; horses need to be entered in the race by 11am and led out between noon and 1pm; and the race must be completed in its entirety by 2pm.

Running at all Costs

It was not until 1619 that a group of 49 fox-hunting gentlemen subscribed the sum of £365 to ensure that the Derby would continue every year – part of the tradition also stipulates that if a year is missed then the race must stop forever. So it was that despite heavy snowdrifts in 1947, Mr Stephenson from Londesborough Wold Farm walked

A Good Day Out

More exciting than a flat race or even the point-to-points held at this time of year, the Kiplingcotes Derby is great fun for spectators. It costs nothing to watch but don't expect Royal Ascot – there are no grandstands, facilities or bookmakers.

Unusually, the rider of the horse coming in second can sometimes receive a higher amount than the winner, as the runner-up prize is made up of the sum of all the entrance fees.

and rode his horse along the course. He was the sole entrant and Harry Ruston, the Clerk of the Course, the sole spectator. In 2001 Ken Holmes defied foot-and-mouth restrictions in order to keep this prestigious East Yorkshire race alive, and in 2006 Derby veteran Ken, by then 74 years old and with ten wins under his belt, ran his last race, earning himself the nicknames Galloping Grandad, Mr Kiplingcotes and even Rebel Rider in the process.

Completing the Course

The course is a gruelling one, and, between the moss-covered starting stone on the grass verge in the parish of Etton and the finish at Londesborough Wold Farm – a distance of 4 miles (6km) – entrants are expected to run along a roadside verge 160ft (49m) above sea level, climb over Goodmarsham Wold to 368ft (112m), drop to Enthorpe Bridge at 303ft (92m) and rise again to a height of 438ft (134m) before tackling the final furlong in thick mud. Hazards encountered on the way include crossing two country lanes, a steep drop before negotiating a disused railway bridge and negotiating the main Driffield to Market Weighton road just before the final straight.

Riders keep up traditions at Kiplingcotes Derby

Tichborne Dole

The custom of the Tichborne Dole was begun in the 13th century by Lady Mabella (her name is also recorded as Maybela, Mabel and Isabella), wife of Sir Roger Tichborne. On her deathbed, Lady Mabella, who was crippled with a wasting disease, asked her husband if he would grant her means to leave a bequest to the village. It was to take the form of a dole (charitable gift of food) of bread to be distributed to any poor folk who applied for it at the manor house on Lady Day. Sir Roger, a heartless man, agreed to give the corn from as much land as his dying wife could walk around while holding a lighted log collected from the fire. Although unable to walk, Lady Mabella succeeded in crawling around a 23-acre (9ha) field (which is still called the Crawls) before the log burned out. Returning to her deathbed, she then prophesied that the House of Tichborne would fall if the custom were to end – the penalty being a generation of seven daughters, thus causing the family name to die out. Not content with this, Lady Mabella also predicted that the ancient house would collapse.

Tichborne House

King Edward the Elder first identified the manor of Tichborne in a grant of land to Denewulf, Bishop of Winchester, in 909AD and the Tichborne family has held the manor since the 12th century. The original house was in existence at least by the year 1293. It is from the porch of the present house, built in 1803, that the head of the Tichborne family traditionally hands out the dole after a blessing by the village priest.

> **The Tichborne Claimant**
> *During the 19th century, an heir to the Tichborne family was believed to have been lost at sea on his way to Australia – but some years later a man arrived in England claiming to be that missing heir. There was a trial in the High Court to establish the identity of the claimant, who was found to be an impostor. Victorian controversy raged over the case, and the Gilbert and Sullivan opera* Trial by Jury *is said to be based on the story.*

Prophecy Fulfilled

Towards the end of the 18th century, Dole Day became a very rowdy affair, attracting the dissolute and dishonest from far and wide. This, at least, was the belief of the local gentry and magistrates and in 1796 the dole was temporarily discontinued. Local folk, however, remembered the final part of the Tichborne legend and when part of old Tichborne House fell down in 1803 it was seen as an ominous portent. The curse seemed to have been fulfilled when Sir Henry Tichborne produced seven daughters but no male heir and the Tichborne estate passed to a cousin, Henry Tichborne of Frimley. It was therefore thought prudent that the charity should continue and all has been well ever since.

LADY DAY

Lady Day is also known as the Feast of the Annunciation of the Virgin Mary (25 March being exactly nine months prior to the birth of Christ) and in Roman times was the first day of the new year.

Before the Reformation, the four quarters of the year were marked in the Christian calendar (some were the result of blending both Christian and pagan festivals). Quarter days marked all sorts of secular events: rents and lease payments were due, taxes were collected and periods of hire of labourers began and ended.

The four quarter days in England, Wales and Ireland are Lady Day (25 March), Midsummer (24 June), Michaelmas (29 September) and Christmas Day (25 December). Those who paid rent half-yearly did so at Lady Day and Michaelmas. In Scotland the traditional quarter days (also known as term days) were different and, until new legislation in 1990, always fell on Candlemas (2 February), Pentecost (50 days after Easter, usually mid-May), Lammas Day (1 August) and Martinmas (11 November).

TAX BREAK

When England adopted the Gregorian calendar in 1752 it was necessary to 'lose' 11 days. It just so happened that in the following year taxes were due on the 25th, which was a Sunday, and so, for religious reasons, they would have had to have been collected on the Monday (26 March). In order to avoid complications the date was therefore postponed by 11 days – making the taxes due on 6 April, which is where the financial year begins and ends to this day.

EASTER CUSTOMS

Easter is an annual festival commemorating the resurrection of Jesus Christ. Easter Sunday always falls on the Sunday after the first full moon following the vernal or spring equinox, which, depending on the year, could be anywhere between 22 March and 25 April. Before Christianity, Easter celebrated Eostre, a Saxon goddess of fertility.

The traditional Easter customs of tossing pancakes, eating hot-cross buns and decorating eggs (and in some cases throwing them down a steep incline for no apparent reason) are well known and the origins of most are covered somewhere in this book.

Eggs, along with rabbits and hares, are recognized symbols of Easter as they represent spring, new life, resurrection and fertility.

HARES AND EGGS

The hare is an interesting one: it has always been known as a mystical creature, able to change its form at will. Indeed, it was thought that witches could turn themselves into hares (Lyddie Shears, a famous Wiltshire witch, was shot and killed by a silver bullet while in such guise). But despite its importance in worldwide mythology and as a harbinger of spring, the hare's place in Easter customs has been taken by the 'Easter bunny' – a continental custom first mentioned in the 1700s and one that has no real significance other than the rabbit's famous ability to breed, thus suggesting new life.

Up until the 4th century eggs were consecrated and used in church ceremonies but after a sudden change in the Church's thinking – due, no doubt, to past pagan associations – their use became forbidden during Lent. This fact didn't seem to put people off hard-boiling hens' eggs and decorating them with symbols such as crosses, churches or fish (the symbol of the early church) as presents for children on Easter Sunday.

PACE-EGGS

In some places in the northeast of Britain Easter eggs are known as pace-eggs. Pace-Egg Day is traditionally Easter Monday; on this and the following day it used to be the custom to roll hard-boiled eggs, coloured in various ways, and use them as playthings. Easter Monday was called Troll-Egg Monday in the neighbourhood of Pickering, North Yorkshire. In former times Paste-Egg Day was applied to Easter Day itself, and among country folk the five latter Sundays of Lent plus Easter Day were called respectively by the names Tid, Mid, Miseray, Caning, Palm and Paste-Egg Day.

Sometimes pace-egging would take the form of groups of men wandering around the locality, one of whom would have blackened his face with soot and be carrying a basket; the idea being that he and his happy band of followers would persuade villagers to throw boiled eggs into it. When the pace-eggers had received sufficient quantities, they would stop and perform either a short play or dance. More often than

not these stops happened to be outside the local inn or the home of a person known to be generous in their hospitality! Meeting a rival band could lead to a fair amount of banter and attempts to steal each other's basket of eggs.

CLAPPING ON ANGLESEY

During the week before Easter children on the island of Anglesey off the coast of North Wales would go around their village begging or 'clapping' for eggs (the custom was known in Welsh as *Clepian Wyau*). They often carried wooden egg-clappers and chanted a little rhyme as they went: 'Clap, clap, gofyn wy, i hogia' bach ar y plwy' (Clap, clap, ask for an egg for little children of the parish). Children might collect as many as 150 to 200 eggs each and these were later displayed proudly on the dresser at home, with the eggs belonging to the eldest child being placed on the top shelf, those of the second child on the second shelf, and so on.

Despite facing strong opposition from 19th-century school teachers who deplored the detrimental impact on school attendance, the custom of clapping for eggs remained popular. Indeed, by the early 1900s members of the teaching profession appeared to have resigned themselves to the fact that few if any children would be present in the days before Easter and so the custom became formally celebrated by the inclusion of an official school holiday.

Palm Sunday

On Palm Sunday (the Sunday before Easter) the villagers of Leafield, Oxfordshire, traditionally went into the Wychwood Forest to a spring called Worts Well, or Uzzle, taking with them bottles containing a spoonful of brown sugar, a piece of liquorice and a black peppermint. They filled the bottles with water at the spring and the resulting concoction was used as a general cure-all.

The local clergy did not approve of the custom and would give small rewards to any children who attended church that day instead of going to the forest.

MAUNDY THURSDAY

Maundy Thursday, the day before Good Friday, is the day on which Jesus celebrated the Passover with his disciples, sharing what has since become known as the Last Supper. In biblical times it was usual for a servant to wash a guest's feet on arrival, but on this occasion there were no servants present and so Jesus washed his disciples' feet, thereby giving them a lesson in humility and service. This act has since been followed, sometimes quite literally, throughout history and used as a reminder that kings and queens were put on this earth to serve their people.

ROYAL CONNECTIONS

It seems to have been the custom as early as the 13th century for members of the royal family to take part in Maundy ceremonies, to distribute money and gifts, and to recall Christ's simple act by washing the feet of the poor. In the 18th century this practice was discontinued and in the 19th century money allowances were substituted for gifts of food and clothing. Henry IV began the tradition of relating the number of recipients of gifts to the sovereign's age, and as it was the custom of the monarch to perform the ceremony, the event became known as the Royal Maundy.

Today's Royal Maundy Thursday Service is held at Westminster Abbey on even-year dates and other abbeys or cathedrals throughout the country on odd-year dates. The ceremony follows pretty much the same format as it did generations ago, with the sovereign distributing specially minted coins to a number of male and female pensioners – one man and one woman for each year of the sovereign's age. The money is contained in two purses, one red and one white. The white purse contains specially minted coins – one for each year of the sovereign's life. The red purse now also contains money, in lieu of the gifts formerly offered to the poor.

Everyone who participates in the service carries posies or nosegays of flowers as traditionally their fragrance would have protected the sovereign from the smell emanating from the unwashed masses. The flowers were also thought to protect the carrier from disease, especially during the time of the Great Plague.

Maundy Money

A complete boxed set of Maundy coins contains a groat (4p), a threepence (3p), a half-groat (2p) and a penny (1p), totalling a florin (10p), but it was not until 1670 that a dated set of all four coins appeared. Maundy money as such started in the reign of Charles II with an undated issue of hammered coins in 1662. Prior to this, ordinary coinage was used for Maundy gifts, silver pennies alone being used by the Tudors and Stuarts for the ceremony. Although today's coins are legal tender, they are generally regarded as collector's items and as such are quite valuable: a groat minted in 1853, for example, may fetch as much as £700 at auction, although a more realistic average for the majority is around £25.

World Marbles Championships

Don't be fooled into thinking that the childhood sport of marbles you may have enjoyed in the school playground is anything like the games played at Tinsley Green – this is a serious contest as befits any form of world championship and has its own rules, rituals and vocabulary. Anywhere else you would be greeted with a bewildered look were you to mention 'nose-drops', 'knuckling down', 'fudging' and 'cabbaging', but at The Greyhound pub you will be immediately understood.

Although marbles have been played in the area for many years, international marbles matches originated some time in the 1930s. Their tremendous popularity is no doubt a result of interest in the game shown by the thousands of Canadian and American servicemen who were stationed in the vicinity during and immediately after World War II.

Around 20 teams compete annually. Forty-nine marbles are placed in the centre of the concrete ring and players receive a point for each marble their 'trolley' (a shooting marble) knocks out of the ring. The first team to reach 25 points is the winner.

Game of Love

Tradition has it that the local interest in marbles stemmed from Elizabethan times when two men from Surrey and Sussex competed for the hand of a young Sussex maiden. After being judged equal in the competitive sports of the day such as wrestling and archery, another sport was needed as a 'decider', and one of the men came up with the idea of a game of marbles. Records fail to reveal whether or not the winner married the girl.

FURMITTY

On Good Friday the people of Abbotsbury in Dorset partake of 'furmitty'. To make the dish in orthodox fashion takes some time. First, wheat is soaked in water for a day or two, after which the outer coat of the wheat rises to the top and the pure corn is extracted. Next the corn is put into the oven to 'cree' (ferment) for two or three hours. After this time the corn is transferred to a pan and milk, sugar, currants, raisins, sultanas, nutmeg or other spices are added. The pan is put on the fire or stove to boil and the brew is then cooked slowly until the milk-coloured substance resembles rice pudding. It is, according to those in the know, extremely alcoholic as a result of the fermented wheat and it was while drunk on furmitty that Michael Henchard sold his wife to a sailor in Thomas Hardy's classic tale *The Mayor of Casterbridge*.

Britannia Coconut Dancers

Bacup, Lancashire (Easter Saturday)

Every Easter Saturday, no matter what the weather, the Britannia Coconut Dancers, with their blackened faces, white plumed turbans, black jerseys, red-and-white kilts, white stockings and heavy Lancashire clogs, manage to stop the traffic of Bacup. Led by the Whipper-In and accompanied by the Stacksteads Silver Band, they dance between the town boundaries.

Also known as Nutters (because of the coconut connection rather than their outlandish clothing), the dancers tap out rhythms on wooden discs or 'nuts' fastened to their palms, knees and waist.

Pirate Dances

This is the sole surviving troupe practising the five garland dances and two nut dances thought to have been brought to Cornwall by the Moorish pirates who settled and became employed in the mining industry. As mines and quarries opened in Lancashire in the 18th and 19th centuries, some of the pirates' descendants moved north, taking with them both

their expertise in mining and the dances.

The tradition of blacked-up faces could come from the mining connection, but it is more likely to have been a way of preventing the dancers from being recognized by evil spirits. It was also a commonly held pagan belief that for magic to be effective the spell-casters had to be in disguise.

The Coconut Dancers, or Nutters, perform their curious dance

Dinas Bran Pilgrimage

Llangollen, Vale of Clwyd, Wales (Easter Sunday)

Hills and mountains have long played an important role in the observance of country customs. In many parts of Wales the celebrations on Easter morning begin before sunrise with a procession to the top of a nearby mountain, from which the crowds watch the sun 'dance' as it hopefully (but, knowing the weather in that part of the British Isles one can never be too certain) rises through the clouds in honour of the resurrection of Christ. At Llangollen villagers used to greet the arrival of the sun's rays on the top of Dinas Bran, a conical hill, by performing three somersaults, but nowadays it is sufficient to take part in the pilgrimage procession.

The fortress ruin of Dinas Bran towers some 750ft (229m) above the Vale of Llangollen and was occupied in the Bronze Age. It later formed part of an Iron Age hillfort and was then the site of a 13th-century castle power-base for the Welsh princes of northern Powys.

Weather Forecast

In some areas, a bowl of water would be carried to the top of the nearest hill in order to catch the reflection of the sun 'dancing' on the horizon: if the sun glimmered it would be wet on that day, and if it shone bright and clear in the water it would be fine. But a more important prognostication was always made when the day ended, for it was understood that if it was fair on Easter Day there would be a fine harvest following it, while if the morning were wet and the afternoon fine, the 'fore-end' of the harvest would be wet and the 'back-end' fine, and vice versa.

Hare Pie Scramble and Bottle Kicking

Hallaton's bottle game stems from the mid-18th century, but the hare pie scramble is, according to Christina Hole writing in her book *British Folk Customs* (Book Club Associates, 1976) 'probably of mediaeval origin, though no one now knows when it actually began'. No two accounts seem to agree on its derivation, which range from two women being saved from a charging bull by the intervention of a hare, to the provision of hare pies, beer and penny loaves as settlement on a piece of land used by the clergy. One thing that most concur with, however, is that at its inception the remains of a hare pie were taken to Hare Pie Hill where they were spread on the ground – probably as some kind of fertility ritual from the Dark Ages when a hare would be sacrificed in honour of the goddess Eostre.

In 1790 the vicar of Hallaton attempted to ban the event because of its non-Christian origins but he was forced to back down when the threatening message 'No pie, no parson' mysteriously appeared on the wall of his home.

The vicar of Hallaton blessing the hare pie

Villagers proudly carry two of the 'bottles' from the bottle kicking

The Bottle Kicking

Proceedings still begin with the consumption of a large hare pie (rather confusingly now made from beef), but these days the local vicar first blesses the pie. Portions are then distributed among the waiting crowd and the bottle kicking contest between the two villages of Hallaton and neighbouring Medbourne gets under way.

Facing each other, the teams fight over three ribbon-bedecked barrels (bottles), which are each released in turn. During the following few hours every effort is made to either roll or carry the barrels to the two village boundary streams situated a mile apart. There are no rules to the game, which is perhaps better described as a free-for-all and can become quite violent with contestants having to negotiate hedges, ditches, lanes and barbed wire. At the end of the day a scorer announces the winners who are then chaired to the town cross where the real festivities begin in earnest with both teams sharing the beer contained within the final 'bottle'.

World Coal Carrying Championships

When Lewis Hartley mocked his drinking buddy Reggie Sedgewick with the words 'Ba gum lad tha' looks buggered' in Gawthorpe's Beehive Inn back in 1963, little did he realize that he would provoke a challenge that would lead to the creation of the World Coal Carrying Championships. What began as a £10 bet between two friends has become recognized by *The Guinness Book of Records* as the proving ground for the world's greatest coal carrier – or Coil (coal) Humper, to use the local parlance.

Gawthorpe is a tough little place, lying between Dewsbury and Wakefield where the coalfield used to provide much of the area's employment. The nearest pit is closed now, but the yearly battle to become King of the Humpers – or Queen, for in these liberated times the ladies have joined in the game – continues.

Unlikely Winners

Competitors come from near and far and have a variety of occupations. On the whole you would expect coalmen to make the best showing, but window cleaners and farmers have done splendidly in past years. Neither are big men necessarily the automatic winners – 10½ stone (67kg) is considered to be a favourable weight for a competitor. Due to safety considerations a maximum of 30 contestants are allowed in each event – 15 postal registrations and 15 on the day. All entrants except the previous year's winner are allocated a place on a first-come first-served basis.

'Coil Humpers' compete for the title at the World Coal Carrying Championships

Men, Women and Children

The main event, the men's contest, starts at the Royal Oak in Owl Lane from where competitors, each carrying 1cwt (50kg) of coal, have to run close on a mile – 1,108.25yds (1,012.5m) to be precise – before being allowed to drop the sacks of coal at the foot of the maypole on the village green. Initially, any lady contestants were let off rather lightly as all they had to do was run from the bottom of the village to the maypole, carrying a 25lb (10kg) bag: in these enlightened times, however, they now run the same course as the men. In recent years a children's event has been added with classes for three age groups.

Biddenden Dole

Much in the manner of the Tichborne Dole (see page 50), bread – or more usually nowadays, a cake – is given out at Biddenden on Easter Monday. Each cake or biscuit is stamped with a likeness of two sisters, Eliza and Mary Chulkhurst, who were born in 1100. The girls were Siamese twins – joined together at the shoulder and hip – and died within six hours of one another in 1134. The story goes that they left some of their land to the village (still known locally as the Bread and Cheese Lands) to provide money for the poorer villagers. Recipients of the dole, also sometimes called Maids' Charity, must have lived in Biddenden for at least a year.

'Hip-Hop'

Originally, beer was given out as part of the 'dole', but that particular part of the custom ceased in the 1600s. Hops, from which beer is made, have always been a part of Kentish tradition, although when they were first introduced by the Romans (who else!) they were grown as a vegetable.

Like vines used in wine-making, hops produce new growth each spring, which are then trained along wires suspended between posts. Until the last half of the 20th century, hop-picking was a regular source of extra income for many people, who would all travel to Kent each September in search of casual work. They included gypsies and whole families from London's East End, who, as well as being paid, treated the whole adventure as a kind of holiday.

APRIL FOOLS' DAY

The origins of April Fools' Day are not clear, but it seems safe to say that the festival is connected to the old New Year celebrations.

In 1562 New Year's Day moved from 25 March to 1 January (see page 11), but, communications being what they were in those days, many people did not receive the news for several years (or refused to accept it) so continued to celebrate New Year on the old date, with festivities going on for about eight days. These folk were regarded as fools: they were made fun of and tricks and practical jokes were played on them. Other people sent them on a 'fool's errand' or tried to make them believe that something false was true.

In England, joke-playing must be carried out by noon, while in Scotland the fun goes on for two days. The second day is devoted to pranks involving the 'tail end' of the body and so it is called Taily Day – the origin of the 'kick me' sign stuck on someone's back can be traced to Scotland.

Hunt the Gowk

A Scottish country name for a cuckoo is 'gowk,' and in Scotland 1 April was sometimes known as Gowking or Huntigowk Day. Hunting the Gowk involved sending someone on a foolish errand, such as asking him or her to take a hand-written note to another person without reading it. On it would be written: 'Dinna laugh, an' dinna smile, But hunt the gowk another mile.' The recipient of the note then had to think of another way to fool the unsuspecting messenger.

Passing the Penny

If you find yourself in the Pennine village of Helpin on the second Monday after Easter don't be surprised to be asked if you want to 'spend a penny'– it will be in honour of John Marsden, a son of the village who, in 1657, travelled to Oxford in search of education and fortune. Three years later, having worked during the day and gained an education in the coffee houses of Oxford in the evenings, he bought a small farm on the outskirts of Woodstock: in doing so, he amassed sufficient funds to be able to travel the country lecturing on current agricultural practices.

Such was Marsden's gratitude to the inhabitants of Helpin for helping him finance his journey to Oxford that he bequeathed an annual legacy for all village boys of 13 years of age to be given a penny so they might, at least once in their lives, have the opportunity to enter a coffee house in search of education.

Nowadays, the legacy takes the form of 'penny biscuits', which are given to all local children outside The Helpin Arms public house at 11am.

> ## Cheap Education
> In the 17th and 18th centuries coffee houses were often called Penny Universities because of the cheap education they provided – for one penny, anyone could read the newspapers, listen to lectures and engage in discussion on any number of disparate topics. Indeed, the Royal Society is said to have sprung from such a venue and men like Edmund Halley (he of comet fame) were known to have met at 'Jonathan's' in Exchange Alley to compare ideas.

Tuttimen Hocktide Festival

Hungerford, Berkshire (second Monday after Easter)

The Hocktide festival is held in memory of John of Gaunt, Duke of Lancaster and father of Henry IV, who, in gratitude for the hospitality he had received from Hungerford's residents in 1364, gave the town special hunting and fishing rights. These rights have been passed down through the generations.

The Officials

On Hocktide Day a horn is blown at 8am to summon the commoners to an annual court convened to consider the dispensation of these rights. Since 1550 the court has appointed a Constable of the Town and Manor, and although his duties are now more or less ceremonial his presence is still an important one on this particular day of the year.

The Constable has a number of officers to help him, including two ale-testers. This post is believed to have originated in the days when houses in the town used to brew their own beer. One method of testing its quality was for the ale-tester to sit on a puddle of beer that had been poured on to an oak seat – if, after a certain length of time,

A Tuttiman on Hocktide Day

the tester attempted to rise and his breeches stuck to the bench, it was thought that the liquid contained too much sugar to be any good!

The court also elects two Tuttimen who carry long poles decorated with scented herbs, red and blue flowers and ribbons; at the very end of the pole is a spike with an orange on it. The red flowers are supposed to represent the monarch, and the blue the town's colour.

The Duties

The Tuttimen's duties begin with calling on all the houses that have the common right, where they expect to receive money and sustenance. The ladies of the house can choose to either pay the money or give the Tuttimen a kiss.

The exact derivation of the name 'Tutti' is unknown: some schools of thought say it is taken from the term 'tithing', while others think that it comes from the fact that a 'tutti' is the name for the posy used to decorate the Tuttiman's rod of office.

Binding Agreements

Hock Day was when tenants paid certain rents to their landlords (hence the expression 'to be in hock', meaning to be in debt). Half the annual rent was paid on Hock Day and the other half at Michaelmas (see page 52). The old tradition was that Hocktide spanned the Monday and Tuesday of the week after Easter, when women on the Monday and men on the Tuesday would bind members of the opposite sex with ropes, thus committing them to a donation for the church. For that reason the days are known as Binding Monday and Binding Tuesday in some areas of the country. It's possible that Hock Days have an even earlier origin connected with a fertility rite.

At each common right house the Tuttimen hand over an orange from the pole, replacing it with another before moving on to the next port of call. The local schoolchildren used to have an official half-day holiday so that they could follow the Tuttimen on their rounds in the hope of picking up some of the money on offer, but nowadays it seems that they have to content themselves with attending the Town Hall after lessons have finished to pick up coins thrown from the steps. As the local inhabitants say: 'it's not unusual to see children with bandaged fingers in the days following. Fingers get trodden on, toes get trodden on and mums never send their kids out in good clothes to go scrambling for pennies on Tutti-day!'

Children scramble for pennies among the Tuttimen

St George and the Dragon

If you ever have any desire to become a saint, remember that it is obviously a necessary requirement to be martyred first – and poor old George was no exception. St George's Day is celebrated on 23 April, the same date as Shakespeare's 'official birthday' (see page 74).

Other than the fact that St George died this day in Palestine sometime in the 4th century, there appears to be very little known for certain about his life. It is strange though that he became the patron saint of England when his most famous exploit, that of killing the dragon, took place in Asia Minor.

Good over Evil

According to Christian legend, the sheep stocks of a village there were decimated by a dragon, who, having run out of sheep on which to feed, turned his attentions to the villagers – virgin girls in particular. It eventually became the turn of the king's daughter who was chained to a rock in readiness  for the dragon. As is the way of legend, it appears that, fortunately for the princess, St George happened to be passing. However, rather than kill the dragon outright he intimidated the beast into surrendering then led it back to the castle with the princess's girdle. The king was understandably overjoyed at George's triumph and agreed, along with his townspeople, to George's proposal to convert to Christianity – at which point St George eventually despatched the monster.

Due to its moral of good triumphing over evil, the legend has become an integral part of the mumming plays that feature in so many of the customs held at Christmas and the New Year (see page 212).

Different Characters

Interestingly, in the early days of Christianity, it was St Michael rather than St George who first appeared in the legend and it was not until around the time of the Crusades that the story began to feature George.

In pre-Christian times the place of St Michael, St George and their respective dragons (personifying the defeat of evil by the creation of good) was taken by Perseus and Andromeda, or as described in the classic tale of Mithras and Marduk. At that time, the character of the maiden in all the stories was meant to represent the earth goddess who has the power to produce all the fruits of summer, thereby creating a connection not only with St George but also with several country customs that appear in this book.

Shakespeare Procession

The annual Shakespeare Procession has its origins in the mid-18th century when the actor David Garrick held a Jubilee in honour of Shakespeare. It was, however, almost 70 years before another was planned (on the bicentenary of Shakespeare's death in 1816) and a further eight years before the newly founded Shakespeare Club organized the first ever procession through the streets of the town, walking to Holy Trinity Church in order to visit Shakespeare's grave. The procession was followed by a dinner. In 1864 an 11-day celebration was held, during which 2,000 people sat down to dinner and there were concerts, plays, a fancy-dress ball, pageants and brass bands.

Today's Events

Held on the Saturday nearest to the 23rd, the traditional events take the form of a procession to lay floral tributes on Shakespeare's tomb,

---

Birthdays

As every schoolchild knows, William Shakespeare was born on 23 April 1564 and died on the same date some 52 years later – thus sharing his special day with St George. Or at least, so it is alleged, as birth dates were not registered at that time. However, according to the Book of Common Prayer, a child had be baptized on the nearest Sunday, or Holy Day, and as there are records of Shakespeare's baptism on 26 April the date of Gulielmus Filius Johannes Shakespeare's birth is set as 23 April.

---

a birthday luncheon and, in the evening, a performance of one of the Bard's plays. Since the beginning of the last century it has been the custom to invite representatives from other countries and the processional arrangements include the unfurling of national and international flags. Around 600 distinguished guests and local people, including High Commissioners and Ambassadors, attend the luncheon.

There is much for the onlooker to enjoy as the procession weaves its way towards the church. As well as representatives of many countries, civic worthies and leading scholars, the procession features members of the acting profession, brass bands, circus acts, strolling players, Morris dancers and ordinary townspeople, most of whom carry flowers to take to Shakespeare's grave or wear sprigs of rosemary ('for remembrance') in their buttonholes.

Of the 1864 celebration, the *London Evening News* wrote, with amazing arrogance, 'Who are these provincials who dare celebrate Shakespeare in their own town – only London men have the capability of organization.' Despite that particular newspaper's doubts, it appears that the locals have done a good job in the intervening years! Today's events are entirely funded and organized by local effort; the four main sponsors being, The Royal Shakespeare Theatre; the Shakespeare Birthplace Trust, Stratford-on-Avon District Council and Stratford Town Council. Members of each group, together with other local organizations make up the celebration committee and further funding is obtained from businesses in the area. Without their enthusiasm, the procession would, no doubt, have ceased to exist.

Letting the White Bread Meadow

Traditionally, the annual Letting of the White Bread Meadow always took place on the Monday after Palm Sunday, but it is nowadays more often held on a convenient day in April – irrespective of when Easter falls.

In 1742 Matthew Clay, a farmer of Bourne, bequeathed two pieces of land to the village, specifying that the annual rent from it must be used to distribute white bread to the householders and commoners of the surrounding area. The original parcels of land were called the Constable's half-acre and the Dike Reeve's half-acre, but when the Enclosures Act came into being in 1770 the two were combined into a single plot, which eventually became known as Bourne Meadows.

The conditions of letting were that two good loads of manure be put on the land, the fence to be kept in proper repair and that the bush in the middle of the field should not be cut or damaged by either animals or humans (the original bush has disappeared but replacements have always been planted as necessary).

Auction Rules

Clay also stipulated how the new tenant should be chosen: at the auction, two boys are given the signal by the auctioneer to start running along a 100yd (92m) stretch of road situated beside the Queen's Bridge at the end of Eastgate, at which point bidding for the grazing rights begins. This ends when the boys return: the bid made as the race is ending is the final one and the successful bidder becomes the tenant of the land for the following year. Nowadays there is no actual bread involved and the last time that money raised was spent on loaves to distribute to the needy was in the late 1960s. The rent money now goes to a local charity. Originally the boys who ran the race also received one shilling each from the auctioneers.

After the letting has been completed everyone attends a feast of bread, cheese, and spring onions all, of course, washed down with beer. Originally, six pubs in the area took turns in hosting the feast, but nowadays only The Anchor and The Marquis of Granby remain.

Keep it in the Family

Many of the people responsible for organizing the event are from families who have been involved for generations. Some of the stewards are second or third generation, while one auctioneer and chairman of the charity held the post from 1959 to 1994, before being succeeded by his son.

There are however, some new additions to the Letting of the White Bread Meadow, not the least of which is the inclusion of Morris dancing by a local side.

Famous Son

The village of Bourne has a place in history as the birthplace (supposedly) of Hereward the Wake. It was from here that he attempted to prevent William the Conqueror from taking control over the fenland districts of Cambridgeshire. Unfortunately, despite all his valiant efforts, Hereward was killed by Norman soldiers, thereby earning himself the dubious distinction of being the last Saxon chief to resist the invading Norman army.

SQUAB, PARSLEY AND LICKY PIES

You might suppose that, as the term 'squab' is used to describe a young pigeon, Squab Pie would contain pigeon meat – well, not in Devon. If you see the dish on a pub menu in or around the South Molton area you'll find that the meat element is made up of tender lamb combined with apples and onions!

Choose a Parsley Pie, however, and you are on much safer ground: you're likely to be served a quiche-like affair where a couple of handfuls of chopped-up parsley have been laid in a pastry base and covered with eggs and cream before being oven baked. Cold, it can be cut into slices and taken on a picnic.

Another local favourite that can be eaten either hot or cold is the dubious sounding Licky Pie. To make it, line a dish with pastry, boil some leeks and cut them into small pieces before placing them in the pie base together with bacon, egg, cream, salt and pepper. Cover the whole lot with a pastry lid and bake until the top is golden-brown.

If you happen to be in the area at teatime, look out for the traditional honey cake. Containing butter, brown sugar, honey and golden syrup, it is deliciously moist without being at all sticky and is a perfect finish to the traditional Devonshire tea.

MAY DAY CUSTOMS

MAYPOLES

The earliest sources suggest that the maypole acted as a focal point for festivities or games on May Day (1 May), marking the spot where everyone should meet. Although there is no evidence that they were ever connected to pagan beliefs or used as phallic symbols, this did not prevent the Puritan reformers, who were hostile towards all forms of drunkenness, dancing and merrymaking, from banning maypoles almost as a matter of principle.

QUEEN OF THE MAY

The custom with all May Day celebrations was to pick a pretty girl as the Queen of the May and adorn her with flowers and ribbons: she would then lead the ceremonies. Originally there was also a King of the May, a Spirit of Vegetation and several other characters, traditionally adding up to a total of 13 main participants. The King or the Spirit of Vegetation might then feign sleep in a field before being woken by the Queen with a kiss, whereupon the couple danced off into the greenwood to consummate the revival of nature.

Other May Day traditions have taken their cue from this and it was not unusual for fair maidens to roll naked in the foggy dew (the subject of folk songs and adolescent boys' fantasies), or at least wash their faces in the morning dew. Being chosen as the May Queen was not without its disadvantages, as in many cases it was thought that the girl would die within the year.

Height Matters

Barwick in Elmet, Yorkshire, was famous for the height of its permanent maypole – 86ft (26m) – and every three years on Easter Monday it was customary to lower it so that a team of 'polemen' could renovate it.

BELTANE

In Scotland, the pagan fire festival of Beltane on May Day marked the start of the second half of the Celtic year and included elements closely associated with the marking of boundaries as livestock was put out to summer pasture. Birch trees, being one of the first to break leaf, had a particular significance and crosses of birch twigs were sometimes placed over doors on May morning, where they were left until the following year.

A Beltane Festival is still held at Peebles during the summer solstice, while at Calton Hill, Edinburgh, a Beltane fire is lit on the eve of May Day when a Green Man and a May Queen represent fertility and lead the hillside celebrations.

Bannock cakes or bannocks – oatcakes coated with baked-on custard made of cream, eggs and butter – were cooked over open fires and anyone who chose a misshapen piece was likely to suffer bad luck in the coming months. The cakes were also offered to the spirits who protected the livestock.

Carols and Couples

On May Day at 6am the choristers of Magdalene College, Oxford, sing a carol from the top of Magdalene Tower while facing east to the rising sun: the bells of the chapel then ring and Morris men begin dancing in the street to entertain the early-morning crowd that gathers on the nearby bridge.

The residents of Hitchin in Hertfordshire used to greet the day with a procession led by two couples: Mad Moll and her 'husband' and two youths dressed as the Lord and Lady.

Knutsford Royal May Day

Knutsford, Cheshire (1 May)

Knutsford's celebrations on May Day have changed and developed since its inception in 1864 when there were cows and cowmen, sheep and shepherds, milkmaids, village weddings and gipsy kings and queens. Also taking part in the activities were well-known characters – particularly those of the Robin Hood legend, whose personalities had ancient and symbolic connections to May Day. As years went by not only did the event earn its royal title in 1887, courtesy of the then Prince and Princess of Wales, but the distinctly rural style also gradually gave way to much more of a carnival atmosphere.

Early in the morning, the streets are strewn with coloured sand in preparation for the procession, which starts in the afternoon at the Town Hall and follows a route nearly a mile long. The procession includes Morris dancers, veteran bicycles, brass bands, foot guards, ladies-in-waiting and a crown bearer, behind which follows the uncrowned Queen. Leaving from Sessions House, the procession circulates the town via Adams Hill and King Edward Road before heading towards the Heath where the coronation takes place (the crown is eventually given to the May Queen as a keepsake).

Sanding

The custom of 'sanding', although nowadays probably peculiar to the streets of Knutsford, is thought to have its origins in the story of King Canute: legend has it that he wished a wedding couple, 'as many children as there are grains of sand'. The practice of sanding the route over which newlyweds would walk was in existence long before it was adopted for use in May Day celebrations.

'Obby 'Oss Ceremony

Padstow, Cornwall (1 May)

Hobby Horse is a diminutive of Robin Horse (the term Robin once meaning a small or medium-sized horse) and at midnight on May Eve (30 April) the 'Obby 'Oss ceremony begins in the streets of Padstow with the singing of the May, or Morning, Song. The crowds stop outside the various houses along the route demanding that anyone asleep should wake up and join in the festivities.

'Oss Play

Despite these late-night revelries, early on May Day morning the town and its maypole, decorated with greenery, ribbons and flowers, awaits the arrival of the sinister apparition of the 'Obby 'Oss; this is a man

Battle of the Seasons

The 'Obby 'Oss ceremony symbolizes winter having one last fling before summer arrives once more: it is possible that half of the tradition has been lost – the full ceremony either being a clash between the dragon, the 'Oss, and St George, or the horse-headed man of ancient times who represents the waning year and the Green Man (see page 106) who represents the waxing one. Legend has it that the Green Man refused to die, cheating death by changing places with the horse-headed man, and possibly dates from some time in pre-history when human sacrifices were made.

wearing a gruesome mask and a skirt consisting of a wide circular frame covered with black material intended to represent the body of a horse. Originally there was only the one 'horse', known as the Red Ribbon 'Oss, but around 100 years ago it was decided to include another, which has become known as the Blue Ribbon or Temperance 'Oss. The Hobby Horses dance and cavort along the streets with the accompanying crowd singing the Day Song. Attendants called 'teasers' constantly bait the 'Obby 'Osses, which respond by snapping and attempting to trap any pretty girl they see by hiding them under their skirts – tradition has it that anyone caught in this way will become pregnant by the end of the year, so onlookers should watch out! Every so often, one or other of the 'Osses collapses and dies, at which point the crowd sing a sad lament until it suddenly springs to life: they finally die at midnight.

The sinister-looking 'Obby 'Oss on the streets of Padstow

Sweeps' Festival

The annual Sweeps Festival in Rochester is an extravaganza of colour, music and atmosphere. It began with chimney sweeps celebrating their annual holiday on 1 May with a procession through the streets accompanied by the Jack-in-the-Green or Green Man, a symbol of fertility and rebirth used to mark the return of summer and therefore a traditional figure of many May Day celebrations. With the passing of the Climbing Boys Act in 1868, making it illegal to employ boys to clean inside chimneys, the tradition gradually died out before being revived in its present form in the 1980s.

Since then festival has grown in popularity and now attracts many thousands of revellers keen to either participate in the parade or to simply watch and take in the atmosphere.

Meeting Jack

The Jack-in-the-Green awakening ceremony commences at dawn on May Day when local Morris sides greet the 7ft-tall (2m) greenery-clad effigy, and after an hour or so of dancing everyone heads off to the pubs, which have opened early to serve breakfast.

Dance teams from throughout Britain demonstrate a variety of steps and styles while folk bands and other musical groups and singers perform at various venues.

There are also 'sweeps' – usually young children dressed up in costume with blackened faces – collecting for charity. It is considered lucky to be kissed by a sweep, a fact that the black-faced Morris men are quick to cash in on, claiming that it's lucky to kiss them as well.

Cheese Rolling

With any long-established country custom, it is almost impossible to state categorically why and when it started. It is commonly thought that the cheese rolling at Cooper's Hill, for example, has been in existence since pre-Roman times and is part of a heathen fertility festival celebrating the return of spring. This doesn't, however, tie in with the fact that it used to be held at Midsummer, nor with the possibility that it is connected to the maintenance of ancient grazing rights established in the Middle Ages. At Stilton, it appears that their cheese rolling could possibly have begun as a publicity stunt not all that long ago. Interestingly, the Randwick event was considered obsolete and almost forgotten by country writers in the 1970s.

Before specific fund-raising took place, cheeses were often donated by local individuals and, during World War II, when cheese was rationed, a wooden cheese was used instead of the real thing.

Brockworth

Cheese rolling on Cooper's Hill in Brockworth is an old Whit Monday custom now carried out on the spring bank holiday at the end of May. The rolling traditionally took place in the evening, but now commences at midday. A Master of Ceremonies is present: an official 'starter' is appointed prior to the event and begins the race by counting up to four. The cheese is released on the count of 'three', but the competitors are not allowed to chase after it until 'four' has been uttered – this can lead to a fair amount of anticipation and false starts. The race winners (there are four separate downhill races and three uphill ones) get to keep the cheeses and, provided that a particular race is not over-subscribed, anyone can take part in this somewhat dangerous pastime.

Randwick

At Randwick, things kick off in a slightly more sedate fashion than they do at Cooper's Hill: after a blessing, the cheeses – there are normally three of them – are taken for a genteel stroll (or should that be roll?) in an anti-clockwise direction around the local church, after which one of the cheeses is cut into pieces and shared among the onlookers – eat a piece at your own risk, as the consuming of it is supposed to protect one's fertility and ensure future generations. The other two cheeses are kept until the following weekend when they are paraded through the streets accompanied by a Mop Man whose purpose is to 'sweep' the crowds away with a wet mop. He is joined by a Flag Man, a Sword Bearer, two Cheese Bearers, a May Queen and the Mayor: the latter is eventually dipped in the Mayor's Pool – which begs the question as to whether there's any kudos in status. The procession then moves on to Well Leaze, where the cheeses are rolled and chased down the hillside by those mad enough to do so.

Stilton

As for the event at Stilton, locals try and say that the event is 'as old as the village' or that its origins have been lost in 'the mists of time' but on this occasion, no one really knows how far back the tradition of rolling the cheeses goes. Midway through the last century, when the village had turned into rather a quiet place having been by-passed by the A1 and the inns and businesses had seen a big drop in their trade, a landlord of one of the pubs decided to revive an ancient tradition. Apparently! He could be seen rolling a Stilton cheese along the road outside his pub. People came to stand and watch and eventually joined in. And so the sport began – again.

It seems a piece of wood in the shape of a Stilton cheese was produced, a starting line drawn up somewhere between The Stilton Cheese inn and The Talbot inn and the finish line was outside The Bell inn. Brave teams of Stilton men would then vie to roll the cheese to the finish and, after the ensuing scramble, and many tussles and spills, the team that ended up steering the cheese to the finishing line would win. Nowadays, the starting points are outside The Bell and The Angel and the finish is a line drawn at the crossroads between the bottom of Fen Street and Church Street. The prizes are always the same, a whole Stilton cheese and beer for the men and a whole Stilton cheese and wine for the ladies. But, of course, the main prize is to go down in history as a Stilton Cheese Rolling Champion.

The chase is on for the runaway cheese

Furry Dance

Often mistakenly thought to be connected in some way with the floral dance held at Helston each May, in fact this particular ceremony is more correctly known as the Faddy, Ferrie or Furry Dance – the word 'furry' originating from the Latin word *feria*, meaning a feast day. As such, the celebrations almost certainly pre-date Christianity and are meant to express joy at the triumph of spring over winter and light over darkness.

With the arrival of Christianity, pagan activities were frowned upon unless a connection could be made with the bible. Fortuitously for local would-be revellers, it was at Helston that St Michael fought the Devil, thereby justifying the dance.

Dancing the Day Away

The first dance of the day, appropriately enough called the Early Morning Dance, begins at 7am. A couple of centuries ago this would have been the dance of the retainers, domestic help, footmen and butlers. The celebrations continue at 8.30am with a mumming play called the Hal-an-Tow (meaning 'haul on the rope', which is derived from an old sea shanty). Acted latterly by school-children, previously it was performed by adults but gained

Hal-an-Tow Song
Despite the introduction of a verse about St Michael, giving the song nominal religious overtones, the chorus of the song makes it abundantly clear that the festival really celebrates the victory of summer over winter. Other verses relate to Robin Hood, a Spaniard (probably referring to a Spanish raid on nearby Newlyn in 1595) and St George.

such a bad reputation as a drunken revel that it was dropped from the day's proceedings until 1930, when it was revived.

The Children's Dance begins at 10am and there have been known to be as many as 1,000 schoolchildren aged from seven to eighteen participating. The girls traditionally wear white dresses with distinctive garlands in their hair to show which school they come from and the boys wear white shirts and shorts, with bunches of lily-of-the-valley fastened to their shirt fronts.

Perhaps the most spectacular dance is known as the Principal Dance, which sets off from the Guildhall at noon. Seeing the long lines of men and women dressed in top hats and tails and frilly frocks, onlookers might be forgiven for thinking that they have stumbled on a mad cult wedding. The last dance of the day used to be performed by the town's tradesmen, but now the Early-Morning dancers lead it. Anyone who wishes can join in and, like an out-of-control Conga dance, it passes in and out of shops, through people's hallways, down passages – wherever the leaders fancy in fact.

Dancers in their finery for the Principal Dance

Planting the Penny Hedge

For several hundred years a small chapel belonging to Whitby Abbey stood tucked away in the woods close to the River Esk. Described in 1762 as being a 'poor mean structure covered in thatch situated in a damp place', it was the source of one of Whitby's oldest customs, the Planting of the Penny Hedge.

Crime and Punishment

On 16 October 1159 three local men out hunting wild boar in the woods drove one particular animal to take refuge in the chapel, which happened to be the home of a hermit monk. In keeping with his religious upbringing and also being a kindly soul, the monk hid the boar in his cell and refused to let the hunters in to kill the animal. Naturally a little miffed that they looked likely to go without a meat course at their next banquet, the hunters decided try and force their way in and beat the monk severely with their hunting staves. He was so badly injured that he later died from his injuries, but not before telling the tale to the Abbot of Whitby and begging that the men not be prosecuted – on condition that they should pay for their sins. The penance was that on sunrise on the eve of Ascension Day every year these men and their successors should collect a number of short staves from Eskdaleside. They then, without the aid of servants, had to carry them to Whitby and at precisely 9am were to plant the staves in the mud in the harbour and weave a small hedge strong enough to withstand three tides. If the hedge collapsed before three tides had come and gone then all the lands belonging to these three men or their successors would be forfeited to the Abbot of Whitby.

Things were not all bad, however, as there was a clause that stated that if ever the tide prevented the planting of the Penny Hedge then the penance should cease. History has since proven that the descendants of the Hutton family (the original hunters) performed the ceremony for over 800 years until, in 1981, the site was covered by 8ft (2m) of sea water and the family members were released from their obligation.

Despite this, the ceremony continues by the harbour opposite The Middle Earth tavern on the morning of the eve of Ascension Day. At the end of the ceremony, a 500-year-old horn is blown and the Bailiff of the Manor shouts the rebuke 'Out on ye! Out on ye!' – the words uttered by the hermit monk as the boar hunters entered the chapel.

Planting the Penny Hedge continues in Whitby to this day

BLESSING THE SEA

Our god-fearing ancestors were well known for their superstitions, myths and legends. Folklore provided explanation for events beyond reason, or those simply feared. Particularly renowned for their superstitions were seafarers, ever hopeful of attracting good luck or avoiding bad.

- *Whistling up the wind is considered unlucky, thereby summoning a gale that may lead to the loss of the boat.*

- *Blood spilt at sea will turn away the whitefish shoal.*

- *Mackerel should be eaten from tail to head or fish will turn their heads to escape the nets.*

- *Seagulls are believed to be the souls of lost seamen.*

The custom of Blessing the Sea is a relatively modern one in Britain, although in Europe and out in the Hebrides or on the west coast of Ireland it has been carried out for generations. There is, however, evidence that similar festivals were held around the coasts of Britain by local guilds well before the English Reformation – after which they appear to have been largely abandoned. Similar festivals were started up again in the 19th century and are nowadays usually celebrated on Ascension Day.

Rogation Day and Beating the Bounds

The name Rogationtide, or Rogantide, derives from the Latin word *rogatio*, to intercede, ask or beseech. It's traditionally a time when prayers are made for God's blessing on the land, livestock and crops in the hope of a good harvest. At an ancient Roman festival called Robigalia people went into their fields and prayed to the gods to protect their crops. As Christianity spread through Europe, the festival continued, but the Church did not adopt it until the late Middle Ages. The fifth Sunday after Easter was fixed in the liturgical calendar as Rogation Sunday, and the following three days leading up to Ascension Day as Rogation Days.

Beating the Bounds

The custom of Beating the Bounds at Rogantide has taken place in a variety of forms for over 2,000 years and in essence involves local inhabitants walking around and inspecting their property, beating certain trees, walls and hedges that mark the boundaries with sticks. The ceremony might also involve the blessing of crops or animals and the inspection of fences.

Trees and other landmarks along the boundaries were noted as places for prayer, preaching or bible readings, leading to the eventual naming of places such as Gospel Oaks or Gospel Thorns, Amen Corner, Luke Stone or Epistle Field. Stone crosses were sometimes erected at intersections with other parishes.

HARSH LESSONS

From a secular point of view, it was crucial that the demarcations between neighbouring communities were clearly recognized to avoid boundary disputes. Ceremonial processions were an important way of defining both the rights of tenants and the feudal power of the landowner and his agents. One of the best ways of doing this was to take young children around the boundaries and to forcibly instil into them the demarcation lines. Adolescent boys might be hit with willow wands, thrown over hedges into brambles or ponds or, where a boundary had been built over, be required to climb up chimneys or over roofs. Young boys were held upside down and had their heads bumped on a marker stone or 'bound stone' at certain points around the boundary. Bread and cheese and were also given out to ensure the event was remembered by those who took part.

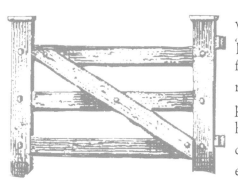

In Dorset a tradition continues whereby boys and girls are given 'points and pins'. By pricking their fingers, they would be encouraged to remember the bounds of the town parish. In 1778, it was recorded that halfpennies were thrown to boys. This custom continues today, unchanged except for the modern coinage.

Border Strife

In Scotland and Wales, particularly in the border towns, ceremonies called Riding the Marches, Riding the Fringes or Common Riding occur with a similar purpose. The term 'marche' derives from the Saxon word for border or boundary. Historically, lawlessness was rife in these border areas and during the 1700s it became necessary to conduct regular inspections to ensure there had been no incursions involving the grazing of cattle or cutting of turf.

Scorton Silver Arrow Tournament

The Scorton Silver Arrow Tournament is a serious archery match organized by the oldest sports club in Britain. Nowadays most competitors use modern state-of-the-art bows made from the most up-to-date materials, but there are still classes where only the traditional wooden longbow is allowed.

Although the event moves to a different location every year, it has its origins in Scorton, near Richmond in North Yorkshire, and is always held sometime in May. First recorded in 1673, it has the distinction of being the world's longest established and oldest recorded sporting event.

Opinions vary as to how the contest begun. One theory is that the original silver arrow was won by the son of the wealthy Waistell family while at Cambridge University in 1653, who then brought it back home to Scorton Manor. Another theory involves a silver arrow reputedly presented by Queen Elizabeth I to a Roger Ascham at the English Archery Championships, most probably held near his house at Oxford. The arrow then found its way to Yorkshire via Ascham's second home at Kirby Whiske (only a few miles away from Scorton).

Chequered History

Over the 340-or-so-year period that it has been known to exist, the silver arrow has suffered a number of indignities, including being gilded, stolen, pawned, mislaid and accidentally left on a park bench. Now housed with the Royal Armouries in Leeds, it is removed only on this one day of the year. The tournament winner is presented with a replica, which they retain for one year, and becomes Captain of the Arrow – a dubious honour as it means they have to organize the following year's event.

Woolsack Race

The annual Woolsack Race in Tetbury probably began (as is often the way with these things) when a group of local men, undoubtedly more than slightly inebriated, set out to impress the local ladies with their strength and athleticism.

Woolsack Day has been an annual event in Tetbury for centuries and is the sole surviving link with the town's once-lucrative wool trade. Though the races have taken place on May bank holiday only since 1973, they are based on a tradition that goes back to at least the early 17th century. At this time young drovers would show off their manliness by racing up Gumstool Hill, which led up from the town's wool market, while carrying a heavy woolsack on their back.

The modern races involve competitors carrying a 60lb (27kg) sack of wool up and down the same steep hill situated between The Royal Oak and The Crown public houses, approximately 280yds (252m) apart.

Today's competitors can take part in a relay event or, if they are really tough, run the individual race. To reflect the sexual equality of modern times, today's event features ladies' races for both individuals and teams – though female competitors carry a lighter load (35lb/16kg) than their male counterparts. There is also a youth race for 16- to 18-year-olds, and they too run with the lighter load. The day's events include a street fair, entertainment, a market, a craft show and a charity auction.

Scolds Beware

Gumstool Hill, with a 1-in-4 gradient, is named after the stool at its foot used in medieval times to dunk suspected witches and nagging wives in the pond.

Hunting of the Earl of Rone

Combe Martin, Devon (Spring bank holiday weekend)

Over four days of the spring bank holiday weekend grenadiers, a Hobby Horse, a Fool and about 500 of the villagers of Combe Martin undertake a search for the 'Earl of Rone'. He is finally located on the Monday evening when he appears on a donkey, only to be shot by the grenadiers. Fortunately for the Earl, their aim seems to be poor and he is miraculously revived by the Hobby Horse and the Fool and remounted on his trusty donkey. Unfortunately, his escape from death is short-lived and it is not long before he succumbs to more attacks from the grenadiers and is taken down to the beach and thrown into the sea.

The character of the Earl of Rone and his story seem to be based on a certain Hugh O'Neill, Earl of Tyrone. Forced to flee from Ireland in 1607, he was subsequently shipwrecked off the Devon coast. After hiding in the local countryside he was eventually caught by a battalion of soldiers based at a camp just outside Barnstaple. Why the legend should ever have materialized is unclear, as it would appear that the Hugh O'Neill in question went directly to Spain where he died of natural causes.

WELL DRESSING

(Held mainly in May at upwards of 60 locations in and around Derbyshire, although the well-dressing season officially runs from May until September)

Well dressing almost certainly dates back to pagan times. Water was such a vital commodity for ancient man that settlements were always located close to a good supply. The consequences of the source running dry were dire, so, in the absence of insurance brokers (who nowadays would have no doubt have declared it an Act of God, but would have been short of a get-out clause in these pre-Christian times), sacrifices were made to water gods to ensure they did not. The offerings originally took both human and animal form, but eventually these barbaric rituals gave way to the hanging of garlands of flowers over the wells.

IN AND OUT OF FAVOUR

Unusually, it seems that the early Christian Church did not object to the practice of well dressing despite its pagan origins. However, future generations were not so tolerant and for many years the custom was banned altogether. During the reign of Henry VIII the Chancellor, Thomas Cromwell, was instructed to arrange the destruction of all the equipment used in well dressing. At Buxton the statue of St Anne, the mother of the Virgin Mary, was dismantled and the crutches and sticks of those who had visited the well in the hope of having their disabilities cured were smashed.

Well dressing still maintains strong Christian links and many of the scenes depicted have a religious significance and a religious (usually inter-denominational) ceremony is performed to bless the wells.

Some well dressings commemorate the period of the Black Death in 1348–49, when probably a third of the population of England died of the disease. At Tissington, the village inhabitants remained healthy and attributed this to their clean water supply.

Dressing Wells

Dressing a well begins with a wooden board, which is thrown into the local river to soak for a few days before being hauled out and covered with soft, wet clay. The next job is to transfer the outline of the picture to the clay, and every village has its own way of doing this. Some use wool; others use peppercorns, bark or alder cones, known locally as 'blacks'. Then the picture is filled in with flowers. Some villagers call this 'petalling' but in Holymoorside it is known as 'flowering' because whole flower heads are used. Dressing a well can take a team of people up to seven days to complete – about the same time as the finished article lasts, before the clay dries and cracks and the flowers fade.

Garland Day

At Castleton on Oak Apple Day the Garland King and his Lady Consort ride through the town on horseback accompanied by a band, children and Morris men.

> ### The King's Garland
> *The garland, which can weigh some 44lb (20kg), is a bell-shaped frame decorated with locally gathered greenery, flowers and ribbons. Each year one of the local public houses is responsible for building it. There are two eyeholes for the King to see through and the whole contraption is crowned with a posy of flowers known, confusingly, as the 'queen'.*

At 6pm the King and his Lady arrive at the pub where the garland is hoisted on to the mounted King's shoulders, thus completely covering the upper half of his body. The Garland King resembles the Jack-in-the-Green of other customs, and is certainly intended as a symbol of fertility and spring. As it parades around the town the procession stops for a drink at each pub until reaching its last port of call, the churchyard. Here the 'queen' flower posy is taken from the garland and is then hoisted by rope on to the middle pinnacle of the church steeple where tradition maintains that it must remain for three weeks – until every flower is dead. The 'queen' used to be presented to the wife of a local VIP but nowadays it is laid on the war memorial as a bugler plays the Last Post.

Duck Feast

Charlton, Wiltshire (1 June)

Anyone with a passion for *canard à la orange* would be seriously disappointed if they turned up at The Charlton Cat public house on 1 June! Here the duck in question is one Stephen Duck, a poor farm labourer who taught himself to read and then began to write poetry.

Royal Circles

In 1729 Duck was 'discovered' and, much to the chagrin of other, better, poets became the protégé and favourite of Queen Caroline. His work was published in 1730 and includes *The Thresher's Labour*, in which he describes his own farming experiences. Duck enjoyed his success at court for more than 20 years, despite enduring numerous parodies (usually involving his surname) from his rivals.

His Charlton-born wife having died, he subsequently married the Queen's housekeeper, took holy orders, and was given a rich living in Surrey. But he became depressed, and eventually, on a journey back to Charlton in 1756, drowned himself at reading. His memory has been preserved by an annual Duck Feast, originally meant for the benefit of Charlton threshers and financed by the profit from a small plot of land (Duck's Acre) purchased for this purpose by Lord Palmerston in 1734. The feast is presided over by the Chief Duck (sometimes a member of the local Fowle family!), who wears a hat adorned with duck feathers. Toasts are drunk to Lord Palmerston and the Reverend Stephen Duck.

West Linton Whipman Play

This event is one of the older Borders festivals, having originated from the annual agricultural holiday and fair held at West Linton from 1803 when 'the men of Linton for the bettering of themselves and their children, formed a Benevolent Society they being known as the Whipmen of Linton'. (Whipman is the old Scots word for carter, or carrier.)

Thus began a tradition of celebrating the closing of the Society's year by organizing a holiday known as the Whipman Play. The day would begin with Society members, led by a band, riding out of West Linton alongside an elected leader (the Whipman), who carried the Society's flag. Although the route varied, it always included a number of formal visits to several of the larger houses in the area, presumably to thank the wealthy inhabitants for their patronage throughout the year and, no doubt, in the hope of encouraging more financial support in the forthcoming 12 months. The rest of the day was then devoted to various sporting activities and a dinner was held in the evening.

Whipman Week
Today's week-long festival begins on the Friday evening with the appointment of the Whipman and his Lass, and is followed on the Saturday by a horse-ride around the parish boundaries (see page 94). Events during the rest of the week include competitions, sporting events and athletics, and there is also a bonfire, a barbecue, prize-givings and a fair on the last Saturday.

Nettle Eating Contest

Marsham, Dorset (around 18 June)

At Marsham around 18 June an intrepid band of challengers meet at The Bottle Inn and are each given 60cm (2ft) stalks of nettles and an hour to chew them. The winner is the person with the longest length of empty stalk.

It all started as a contest in the 1980s between two farmers as to which had the longest nettles on their land: a Longest Nettle Night was established and contestant Alex Williams brought in a 15ft (5m) specimen declaring that if anyone had a longer one he would eat his – well, wouldn't you just know it, someone had and Alex was forced to honour his promise, thus beginning the annual Nettle Eating Contest.

SUMMER SOLSTICE

At the Summer Solstice (21 June) the sun is at its highest point and therefore takes the greatest length of time to travel across the sky, giving us the longest day of the year. The word solstice has its origins in the Latin word *solstitium*, meaning 'the sun stands still': this must have seemed the case to our early ancestors due to the length of time the sun could be seen on that day.

In Celtic cultures the solstice was celebrated with bonfires thought to add to the sun's energy and thus delay the onset of winter.

Traditionally, European marriage ceremonies owe much to the period around the Summer Solstice. Ancient cultures believed that the sexual union of the gods took place in May, so marriages would be held over until the first full moon in June, which was also the best time to harvest the honey used in making celebratory mead – hence the origin of the word honeymoon.

CELEBRATIONS AT STONEHENGE

In Britain, Stonehenge is the main focal point for solstice celebrations and the main axis of the stones, thought to have been erected between 3000BC and 1600BC, is in perfect alignment with the summer solstice sunrise. For farming communities the Summer Solstice traditionally represented the chance to relax awhile between haymaking and harvest time, but despite the glorious daylight country folk were all too well aware that it was all downhill from that point.

Interestingly, if you're reading this in the southern hemisphere on 21 June, you will of course, be celebrating the Winter Solstice today. Confusing, isn't it?

Midsummer Cushions

Bishops Auckland, Durham (21 June)

The exact origin of the Midsummer Cushion appears to be unknown, but it is likely to have some connection with Flora, goddess of flowers, and the 'cushion' may have originally been some kind of altar.

In Bishop Auckland, a 'cushion' is a three-legged stool covered with clay into which every kind of flower possible is stuck. This is then placed at the corner of a street or busy thoroughfare next to a pewter collecting plate. Traditionally, a young woman will entice people to part with their money that, later in the day, is used to buy the ingredients for making a Tansey Cake, which is served, more often than not, at the Bay Horse Inn. Dancing and festivities follow until the early hours of the morning.

Tansey Cake Recipe

Beat ten eggs and a little salt. Add a pint of cream, about the same quantity of spinach juice and a little tansey juice. This juice is obtained by grinding tansey flowers, leaves and stem in a pestle and mortar. Add 40oz (113g) of Naples biscuits, sugar to taste, a glass of white wine and some nutmeg. Heat the mixture in a pan just long enough to thicken before placing it in a greased dish and baking in a moderate oven, taking care not to let it burn. When browned, turn the cake on to a plate and decorate the top with finely grated orange and lemon peel and dust with sugar.

THE GREEN MAN

The Green Man is a mysterious pagan deity associated with woodlands and wild places and a powerful fertility symbol. He is also known as Green George in mumming plays and the Green Knight in Arthurian legends. Medieval stories involving 'wild' men dressed in leaves who live in the forest and only venture out to take food have also been connected with him. This is the story on which the legend of Robin Hood – a robber and hero dressed in Lincoln green – is based. In some tales he is linked with Herne the Hunter and enjoys the same godlike status. Present-day pagan thought still identifies the Green Man as a symbol of the cycle of life, death and rebirth, thereby showing all the same attributes as John Barleycorn (a mythological figure reputed to travel around the countryside planting grain seeds and the personification of the ale obtained from their harvesting), himself the subject of many folk songs.

Despite the Green Man's pagan origins, his face, with its flowing beard of leaves, is often seen carved into early churches – it was an attempt to incorporate heathen beliefs into Christianity.

JACK-IN-THE-GREEN

The character known as Jack-in-the-Green appears prominently in many of today's May Day celebrations, especially those connected with chimney sweeps such as at Rochester (see page 84). A man would be 'dressed'· with a conical framework of wicker covered with woodland greenery and, like the Green Man, was almost certainly intended to be a representation of summer and the provider of a successful harvest.

Bawming The Thorn

Appleton Thorn, Cheshire (third Saturday in June)

Appleton Thorn village is the only place in England where the ceremony of Bawming the Thorn takes place. Nowadays it is held on the Saturday before the longest day, which means that the ceremony nearly always takes place on the third Saturday in June, but as recently as 30 years ago it occurred on 5 July – Old Midsummer Day.

Local children 'bawming the thorn'

Bawming means decorating, and the custom involves bedecking the hawthorn tree that stands beside the church with ribbons and garlands. It is thought to be an offshoot of the tree at Glastonbury Tor in Somerset and was brought to Appleton by Adam de Dutton, a knight of the Crusades and a local landowner. As the Glastonbury thorn quite literally stemmed from the staff of Joseph of Arimathea, the man who arranged Jesus's burial, there is some religious significance to the ceremony. It includes a procession through the village, dancing and the singing of the Bawming Song.

Guid Nychburris

With the River Nith on two sides and Lochar Moss on another, Dumfries has always been a town with good natural defences. Consequently it was never completely walled but even so a careful eye had to be kept on the boundaries of the burgh lest neighbouring landowners try to hive off land for their own use. Checking the boundaries was undertaken annually by the Provost and other town dignitaries.

This Scottish form of 'beating the bounds' (see page 93) is still carried out as part of the week-long Guid Nychburris (Good Neighbour's) Festival, the highlight of which is the Riding of the Marches on the third Saturday in June. Following a sequence of events laid down many years ago, the day starts at 7.30am with the gathering of horses and riders who then wait for a runner to arrive and announce that the Pursuivant (an officer of the College of Arms) is on his way. Once the message has arrived, they ride out to meet him then all proceed to Ride the Marches and Stob and Nog (mark the boundary with posts and flags) before returning at 12.15pm to meet the Provost and inform him that all is in order – after which the charter is proclaimed. This is then followed by the crowning of the pageant Queen who represents Devorguilla, the last Princess of Galloway, also known as Queen of the South.

Hepworth Feast

Hepworth, West Yorkshire (last Monday of June)

The Hepworth Feast, which started in 1665, commemorates the end of the plague in the village. The disease arrived in a batch of clothes that had been ordered from London. Unpacking the containers, a servant girl could not resist trying on one of her mistress's new dresses – little realizing that it contained fleas carrying the bubonic plague. Unaware that she had contracted the disease, she continued with her duties and in doing so spread the plague throughout the entire village.

Today's feast, combining Morris dancing, processions and brass bands, is both a thanksgiving for the lives of the survivors and a commemoration of those villagers who died.

Hepworth feast

Golowan Festival

The nine-day Golowan Festival is always organized so as to include the saint's day of St John the Baptist (24 June), the patron saint of Penzance (Golowan is Cornish for the feast of St John).

The festival, revived in 1991, is an adaptation of the ancient midsummer fire festival centred on the lighting of fireworks, tar barrels and torches. Towards the end of the evening, local youths would take part in the Serpent's Dance, an activity that necessitated jumping in and out of any flames they happened to be passing. By the late 19th century, however, the pyrotechnics were considered too dangerous and the tradition was discontinued. A Mayor of the Quay would be elected during the celebrations and a midsummer's day fair took place on the harbourside.

Today's festival includes, concerts, art exhibitions, fairgrounds, dancing, folk singing and several themed competitions

The streets of Penzance in full throng for the Golowan Festival

Braw Lads' Gathering

Galashiels, Selkirkshire, Scotland (last week of June)

The town crest of Galashiels shows two foxes trying to reach the ripe fruit on a plum tree. It refers to an occasion in 1337 when, during a border battle between the Scots and English, a few English soldiers strayed from their main troop to in order to gather some of the plums that grew locally in great quantities. Unfortunately they were noticed by a group of Scottish soldiers who attacked and killed them. This event, together with the granting of a charter in 1599, is now marked by the annual Braw Lads' Gathering.

The Highlight

Although there are events throughout Braw Lads' Week, it is the Gathering on the last Saturday that creates the most interest. At 8am the Braw Lad and Lass – who have both been chosen by members of the executive council responsible for organizing the Gathering – receive the burgh flag from the President of the Gathering at the burgh chambers

I Want to be Alone

In nearby Selkirk, Sonter's Day was commemorated every June. Similarly to the Braw Lads' Gathering, a single horseman would ride out from town carrying a banner and begin to ride the boundaries. This flag was believed to be the banner – or at least a descendant of it – carried back from the Battle of Flodden Field in 1513 by the single returning survivor of all the many men who rode out from Selkirk and marched over the border to do battle.

and vow to return it 'unsullied and untarnished' at 12 noon. The couple then lead the mounted riders in a procession consisting of what is known as the Official and the Main Cavalcades to the Raid Stane – a memorial to the bloody happenings of 1337 (rather unromantically situated near the car park beside the present Gala Fairydean football stadium).

Both parties then ford the River Tweed before the Official Cavalcade splits and makes its way to Abbotsford House, the former home of Sir Walter Scott. Here the Braw Lad conveys greetings to the present occupant. While all this is going on, the Main Cavalcade of riders follow the burgh boundaries before meeting up again with the Braw Lad who then leads everyone back across the River Tweed to the Town Cross. Here they participate in the ceremony of the Mixing of the Roses: red and white roses are intermingled with one another by the Braw Lass to commemorate the marriage of Margaret Tudor of England to King James IV of Scotland in 1503.

After the Mixing of the Roses, members of the Braw Lads' Gathering committee participate in a symbolic hand-over representing the granting of the burgh charter in 1599 before the combined Cavalcade then proceeds towards the war memorial, where everyone except the Braw Lad dismounts. At the sound of the church clock striking noon, he lowers the burgh flag as a mark of respect to soldiers who were killed in the two world wars before returning the flag to the burgh chambers.

MORRIS DANCING

Nothing could be more typically English than a group of strangely attired, bell-bedecked and handkerchief-waving men and women dancing on a village green outside an old inn. Oddly, however, Morris dancing has its origins abroad, though how it got its name is less certain. One theory is that the name is derived from 'morisco', the word used to describe the Spanish Moors driven out by Ferdinand and Isabella in the 15th century and forced to travel through Europe in search of a new life. Another possibility is that it comes from the Romany or gypsy culture and that the word Morris is a derivation of Romish.

HOW IT BEGAN

The type of dancing now known as Morris is said to have been introduced into England by the ubiquitous John of Gaunt, but both sword dancing (linked with winter, and death and resurrection rituals) and folk dancing (linked with spring and early summer, and representing the victory of the summer sun over the winter sun) are older than this. Another alternative might be that Morris men were originally beggars performing for money and that their customs of ringing a bell in the hope of getting alms, or clacking together their wooden dishes to show they were empty, were eventually incorporated into the dance. It has also been suggested that the Morris men were poking fun at the Roman Catholic Church, their meretricious dancing being meant to scorn the posturing of the Roman cardinals and bishops.

MUMMERS

Accompanying the traditional Morris teams were the mummers (see page 212), small groups of players who presented short dramatic pieces based on pre-Reformation rituals that had been passed orally from one generation to the next. Their costumes related to the character and were usually highly decorated with brightly coloured strips of paper or ribbons, with tall hats traditionally dressed with long strips of rushes and scraps of fabric. As the teams of Morris men and mummers danced and played their way through the village, most members of the community would give a little something to avoid tempting

bad fortune or displaying bad manners. Nowadays, however, both activities are usually held in one spot – presumably in order to cut down on the lack of drinking time that moving from venue to venue would entail!

Warcop Rush Bearing

At Warcop, on St Peters Day (29 June), the Church of St Columba carries out its ancient rush-bearing festival. Led by a local band, a procession of adults, girls wearing floral crowns and boys carrying rush crosses make their way from the village reading rooms to the church. On the way they stop for refreshments at Warcop Hall. Among the hymns sung at the church service is a special rush-bearing hymn unique to Warcop.

The custom of rush bearing also continues in four other Cumbrian churches: Grasmere (5 August), Ambleside and Great Musgrave (both held on the first Saturday in July) and Urswick (Sunday nearest to 29 September). Traditionally, the children of Grasmere and Ambleside are given a piece of Grasmere gingerbread if they have carried one of the rushes. Some of the festivals are accompanied by children's sports.

Rush Floors

Originally church floors were simply earth and it was commonplace to bury bodies of well-to-do villagers within the church as well as outside in the churchyard. Parishioners would strew sweet-smelling rushes at the feasts of dedication to purify the air. Seating was not provided until the 15th century and since only the gentry could afford cushions for kneeling, rushes were also used as a floor covering. They were replaced occasionally, though little thought was given to cleanliness and they could be left for years.

In Lancashire rush replacement developed alongside the Wakes Week religious celebrations or the church's feast of dedication and thus became an excuse for singing, drinking and dancing.

GÂCHE CAKE
AND BEANJAR

Despite having chosen loyalty to the English Crown at the time of the Norman invasion, the Channel Islands, and in particular, Guernsey, have many French words in their vocabulary and some of the island's older residents still speak a kind of *patois*.

Gâche is a kind of bread/cake, but, confusingly, any kind of pastry can also be called *gâche*; apple tarts, for example, are called *gâche à pommes*. The traditional Guernsey *gâche* is made from plain flour, butter, eggs, candied orange peel, sultanas, milk, brown sugar and yeast. It is, or was, according to those in the know, '... best served with cider from the jug, whilst out hay making'.

For those with a desire for something more savoury, there's beanjar; a sort of *cassoulet* made with a pig's trotters or a piece of beef, haricot beans, dried herbs, onions and carrots. The beans are soaked overnight and then briefly boiled with the meat before being transferred to an earthenware pot (the beanjar), covered with water and cooked in a slow oven for several hours.

In days gone by many Guernsey families would take their beanjar to the local baker on a Saturday evening and place them in the cooling ovens (as no bread was baked on the Sunday). In the morning the cooked meal was collected and the baker was paid per jar. The beanjar dish was often stored and eaten on the Monday as the women were too busy washing clothes to cook and sometimes the remainder was reheated on the Tuesday, because this was ironing day.

Love Feast

Alport Castles Farm, Derbyshire (first Sunday in July)

Although its name might suggest that the Love Feast is connected with 'flower-power' and a 1960s hippy festival, the custom began in the 17th century with a group of Nonconformists: to escape persecution, they met at this isolated farm near Alport Castles to worship in secret.

The simple service, held in a barn with a straw-covered floor and nothing but a few rustic wooden benches, maintains the tradition of taking fruitcake and fresh Derbyshire spring water rather than bread and wine. Hymns are sung unaccompanied by music and the water is passed around the congregation in a two-handled loving-cup.

Despite its remote venue (up a track from Hayridge Farm west of Snake Pass just off the A57) and its seemingly unexciting format, this annual service, beginning at 1.30pm, is generally well attended.

> ### Women's Rights
> *Hannah Mitchell, one of the six women to form the Women's Social and Political Union (later to become known as the suffragette movement) at the Pankhurst's home in Manchester, was born at Alport Castles Farm in 1871.*

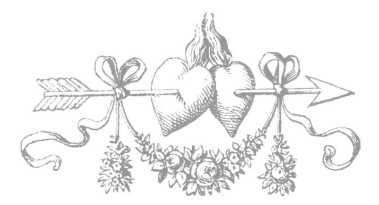

Wenlock Olympian Games

Much Wenlock, Shropshire (first week of July)

Hyped as the home of the modern Olympics, Much Wenlock plays host to the Olympian Games. A local GP, Dr William Penny-Brookes, introduced physical education into British schools in 1850 and was instrumental in creating the Wenlock Olympian Games eight years later. The concept was adopted and developed by various groups throughout the world and ultimately resulted in the first International Olympic Games in 1896, not least because of a visit to the Wenlock games by Baron de Coubertain, an influential and wealthy Frenchman who became one of the founders of the modern, international event. Who knows, 'the old woman's race for a pound of tea' (a real event in Wenlock's sporting past) may yet be reintroduced as an Olympic sport.

Whalton Bale

Whalton, Northumberland (4 July)

A great fire, known as the Whalton Bale, has been built on Whalton's village green in July for generations. 'Bale' is the ancient Saxon word for fire, which itself derives from the name of the sun-god Bel, or Baal. Several other Northumberland villages organize an annual Baal Fire but the majority are held in the winter, unlike the one here, which forms part of the midsummer festival held on old Midsummer's Eve (4 July). The accompanying festivities always include Morris dancers, sword dancing, fiddlers and pipers, and if the date happens to fall on a weekend, the event turns into a massive carnival.

Tynwald Ceremony

St Johns, Isle of Man (5 July)

Tynwald is the name of the island's Parliament and on Tynwald Day all new laws passed during the previous 12 months are read aloud before they actually become law. Traditionally, any subject who objects to their implementation can petition the Lord of Man (the Queen), or, in her absence, her representative – the island's Lieutenant Governor. Part of the ceremony goes back beyond the founding of the Manx Parliament in 979AD; the strewing of rushes along the processional route being a traditional offering made every year to appease Manannan, the Celtic god of the sea.

Up and Down the Hill

The ceremony commences with a church service at the Royal Chapel of St John the Baptist in the village of St Johns. This is then followed by a procession of officials, led by the Lord of Man, to Tynwald Hill, a series of stepped circular grass platforms shaped rather like a wedding cake. Having reached the top of the hill the Lord of Man or her Lieutenant Governor requests that the First Deemster (Chief Justice) directs the court to be 'fenced', meaning that it is in session and that order must be preserved. Next the coroners (officers of the court) are given their staves of office and a public declaration, in both English and Manx, of the laws

The Three Legs
Carved on the back of the Speaker's chair is the island's famous emblem, the Three Legs of Man. The original motif was a Viking ship with furled sails, but it was changed to its present form in 1262. As the island is divided into 'sheadings' (a sheading being derived from the Norse word skeid, meaning ship), there is some logic to the original emblem, but there seems very little to the 'modern' one, which is believed by some to be Sicilian in origin.

The previous year's laws are declared at the Tynwald Ceremony

passed within the previous 12 months is issued. Once the petitioners have been dealt with, the procession makes its way back to the Chapel of St John where the laws are then 'captioned', that is to say they are signed by the Queen (or Lieutenant Governor), customarily with a quill pen, before being counter-signed by the Speaker. Once the formal part of the proceedings has been completed a fair with amusements and market stalls takes place on the field adjacent to the hill.

Kilburn Feast

Kilburn, North Yorkshire (begins on the first Sunday after 7 July)

Take care of your money if you visit Kilburn around this time of the year. On the last day of the ancient four-day feast and fair there is a procession with a mock Mayor and Mayoress (in fact a man dressed in women's clothes). Both try to get money out of bystanders by fining them for the silliest reasons that they can think of.

Dunmow Flitch Trial

Great Dunmow, Essex (every four years, around the second weekend in July)

In the days when it was possible to pronounce oneself 'wed' without the sanction of either a priest or civil ceremony, it was legal to sell your wife provided that both sides were in agreement. Selling your wife would, however, certainly disqualify you from winning the side of bacon on offer at the extraordinary Dunmow Flitch Ceremony held every four years.

The Story of the Trial

Most historians claim that the origin of the Dunmow Flitch dates back to 1104 when the Lord of the Manor of Little Dunmow, Reginald Fitzwalter, and his wife dressed themselves as humble folk and begged blessing of the prior a year and a day after their marriage. The prior, impressed by their devotion, bestowed upon them a flitch, or side, of bacon. Upon revealing his true identity, Fitzwalter gave his land to the priory on the condition a flitch should be awarded to any couple who could, in the future, claim that they were similarly devoted.

By the 14th century the Dunmow Flitch had achieved far-reaching notoriety – even Geoffrey Chaucer alludes to the trials in *The Wife of Bath's Tale*; however, is it not until 1445 that the winners of the flitch were first officially recorded.

In 1832, Josiah Vine, a retired cheesemonger from Reading, and his wife, tried to claim the flitch but the Steward of Little Dunmow refused their request and is reported as saying that he regarded the event as being 'an idle custom bringing people of indifferent character into the neighbourhood'. It was at this stage that the custom was transferred to Great Dunmow. Over the following years the custom lapsed but in 1855, following the publication of Victorian novelist Harrison Ainsworth's novel *The Custom of Dunmow*, in which he recounts the attempts by a Little Dunmow publican to win the flitch by marrying a succession of wives in an attempt to find the perfect one, the Flitch Trials were once again staged in Great Dunmow. Since the end of World War II the custom has been held every leap year.

Court Proceedings

The modern trial takes the form of a court presided over by a judge, with counsel representing the claimants, and opposing counsel representing the donors of the flitch of bacon; there is a jury of six maidens and six bachelors; a clerk of the court records the proceedings; and an usher maintains order.

The court is held in a marquee on Talberds Ley and couples (claimants) married for at least a year and a day come from far and wide to try and claim the flitch. It is not a competition and all couples could, in theory, be successful in their claim.

Lucky in Love
Successful claimants are carried shoulder-high by bearers (traditionally village 'humble folk') in the ancient Flitch Chair to the Market Place where they take the oath (similar to pre-Reformation marriage vows) kneeling on pointed stones. Unsuccessful couples have to walk behind the empty chair to the Market Place and console themselves with the runners-up prize of a piece of gammon.

Eyemouth Herring Queen Festival

Eyemouth Herring Queen Festival, instituted in 1939, followed on from an earlier celebration known as the Fishermen's Picnic. The festival is heralded by a colourful pageant when the town's flag-bedecked fishing fleet escorts the Queen from nearby St Abbs Harbour to Eyemouth. The Queen and her maids of honour are chosen from high-school pupils and the skipper of each fishing boat nominates a girl to be a member of the Queen's court. Their costumes and emblems symbolize the sea and fishing community. After a crowning ceremony the procession tours the town, halting at the war memorial and the memorial to the 129 Eyemouth men lost in a devastating storm on 14 October 1881. A varied week's programme of sports competitions and entertainment follows and the festival is brought to a close with the Fishermen's Service at the parish church.

The Queen and escort at a recent Eyemouth Festival

Sham Fight

In June 1690, King William III (William of Orange), together with his army of some 30,000, camped at the tiny village of Scarva before marching south to meet the forces of the Catholic King James II of England at the Battle of the Boyne the following month.

William himself is said to have camped under a magnificent Spanish chestnut tree, which still flourishes to this day. To commemorate his subsequent victory, a Sham Fight between two horsemen – one dressed as James, the other as William – and a pageant are held annually on the area thought to have been used as a training ground by William's army.

Normally a quiet and peaceful village, upwards of 100,000 people congregate in Scarva on 13 July to watch the re-creation of the battle and parade, which is staged by members of the Royal Black Preceptory, a group closely related to the Orange Order.

Marching Season

Throughout Northern Ireland parades are held to commemorate various battles, including the Battle of the Boyne (12 July), the Battle of the Somme (1 July) and the Siege of Derry (Easter Monday).

What in general is termed the Marching Season runs from around mid-June until mid-August, but in fact parades take place from March through until September. In addition, marching bands have started holding their own local parades. This increased number means that on any Friday or Saturday during the summer months there are probably at least half a dozen marching bands parading somewhere in Northern Ireland.

Church Clipping

Nothing to do with keeping hedges trimmed, church clipping (sometimes spelt clypping) is the custom of encircling the church by holding hands. It probably originates from Celtic times when it was common practice to worship the stone monoliths, menhirs and circles from earlier cultures. There is evidence that the Celts danced around standing stones in a circle holding hands, thus forming an unbroken chain, in the belief that power could be gained from the stone in this way.

Church clipping is more often used as a sign of friendship towards the Mother Church and each other rather than a need to invoke power and strength. It takes place in various counties and at different times of the year. South Petherton in Somerset holds its annual clipping ceremony at Rogationtide (see page 93), for example, and at one time Mothering Sunday was celebrated by church clipping. Despite this, July and September seem the most common months to witness the event.

Countrywide Ceremonies

At Wirksworth in Derbyshire church clipping went out of practice but was restarted in 1921 and nowadays takes place on the Sunday nearest 8 September. After the morning service the vicar, choir and congregation encircle the church by holding hands. A hymn is sung and sometimes there is a procession through the town with church dignitaries in attendance. A similar custom takes place at Burbage Parish Church, near Buxton, on the last Sunday in July.

Saint Oswald's Day (the first Sunday in July) is celebrated at Guiseley Parish Church near Leeds, West Yorkshire, by clipping the church. During the 9.30am service the congregation, led by the choir, churchwardens and clergy, process out of and around the church singing Saint Oswald's Ballad before all joining hands to encircle the church and saying 'God Bless our Church' three times.

Canine Capers

On the Sunday nearest 19 July the townspeople of Painswick (Gloucestershire) clip their church. The 'dish of the day' is Bow-Wow Pie, a fruit pie with a china dog baked in it. Some people claim that the pies were once made with a real dog and one way for a stranger to insult the locals and start a fight in Painswick is to call out 'bow-wow' or imitate the bark of a dog!

In 2000 the Thirties Kids (Painswickians who were at school in the 1930s) carried a banner depicting dogs and pies at the clipping ceremony. Two years later the organizers of the Victorian Street Market (also held in July) arranged with a local supermarket to bake a huge plum pie measuring about 4½ x 3ft (1.4 x 1m).

Ebernoe Horn Fair

Enernoe, West Sussex (25 July)

The Ebernoe Horn Fair is held every year on St James' Day. A centuries-old traditional country fair, it appears to have been revived in 1864 after a long lapse. Some say it began as a pagan fertility rite but it is thought that there are late medieval connections with cuckolds; humiliated husbands being required to parade in public as objects of derision while wearing ram's horns. Centuries ago horn fairs were boisterous events where cuckoldry and seduction would not be unknown. The old saying 'All's fair at Horn Fair' probably originates from such events.

In days gone by it seems that Ebernoe Fair was often beset by thunderstorms. However, these storms were taken as a good luck sign and meant farmers could look forward to a good harvest. The absence of a storm on the other hand suggested the crops would fail. Ebernoe Horn Fair was also the day on which gardeners were reminded to sow their spring cabbages.

Today's celebrations are held on the village common, the main attraction being a cricket match. Towards the end of the day the highest-scoring batsman is presented with a set of horns taken from a sheep roasted earlier in the day.

Cuckoo in the Nest
Cuckold is an old English term for a man whose wife has had an adulterous affair. It relates to the cuckoo – a bird which lays its eggs in another bird's nest.

Swan-Upping

Swan-Upping, the ceremonial business of rounding up swans for marking, dates from medieval times, when the birds had royal status and were regarded as an important part of any banquet or feast. Anyone found either driving away swans at breeding time or stealing their eggs was liable to one year's imprisonment plus a fine. In addition, anyone in possession of a swan hook, by which swans might be taken from the river, was also liable to end up before the 'Beak'!

The Crown could grant the privilege of ownership to others under certain conditions, one of which was that the birds were pinioned and bill-marked in order to establish the identity of the owner. By the 15th century large numbers of swans carried a bill mark and, as these marks were proof of favour with the sovereign, the birds were often used as gifts or bribes rather than as food.

These days the Queen exercises ownership rights on a very small portion of the Thames, with the Dyers and the Vintners companies owning the rest. Formerly, the Worshipful Company of Dyers marked their birds with a nick on one side of the beak, while the Worshipful Company of Vintners placed a nick on both sides, but now they are identified with rings around their legs. The Queen's birds are left unmarked.

Stately Progress
Swan-Upping in the days of Elizabeth I had to be completed by the various game-keepers along the Thames in one day: nowadays, the operation takes place over five, with each leg beginning at 9am. Progressing upstream towards Abingdon, the boats leave Sunbury-on-Thames on the Monday, Eton College boathouse on the Tuesday, Marlow on the Wednesday, Sonning-on-Thames on the Thursday and Moulsford on the Friday. As the boats pass Windsor Castle on the second day, everyone salutes and shouts 'Her Majesty the Queen, Seigneur of Swans'.

Swan Welfare

In today's annual ceremony the Queen's Swan Marker, dressed in a scarlet uniform, together with the Swan-Uppers of the Vinters and Dyers, use six traditional rowing skiffs to carefully manoeuvre birds towards the banks and gently lift them into the boats for inspection and marking. Afterwards the Swan Marker (nowadays more of a scientific than ceremonial appointment) produces a report, providing data on the number of swans accounted for, including broods and cygnets. In addition to this he advises regional organizations throughout the country on swan welfare and incidents involving swans, monitors the health of local swan populations and briefs both fishing and boating clubs on how best to work with wildlife and maintain existing natural habitats. He also coordinates the removal of swans from stretches of the River Thames used for summer rowing regattas – a task that, it might be supposed, is easier said than done.

Swan-Upping on the Thames

GROATY DICK AND FILBELLY

Groaty Dick, or Pudding, is a substantial casserole, originating from the West Midlands, made from shin of beef, onions, leeks and groats – oats before the husk has been hulled. In poor families any cheaper cuts of meat or even pieces of bacon from the family pig would have gone into the dish, which stood simmering on the kitchen grate.

A meal of Groaty Dick may well have finished off with a piece of Filbelly – the local name for bread pudding. Wasting food was bad household management so any stale bread left at the end of the week would be used up; the recipe also included sugar, suet, fruit, eggs and mixed spice. Once mixed together, the ingredients were placed in a greased baking tin and baked in the fireside oven for about two hours, or until nicely browned.

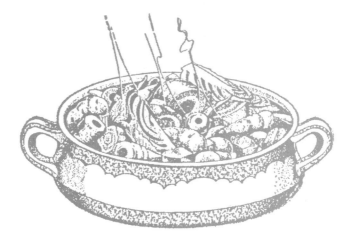

Bonsall Hen Race

Bonsall, Derbyshire (first Saturday in August)

In its current form this is one of the more modern country customs, as it began less than a couple of decades ago when the landlord of the local Barley Mow public house decided to change the format of the hen races traditionally held throughout Derbyshire. Up until then, these had been based on the first hen to lay an egg rather than cross a finishing line.

Contestants and Rules

Also known as the World Hen Racing Championships, any breed of hen is eligible for the Bonsall Hen Race. Former contestants range from the common-or-garden Rhode Island Red to the rare Derbyshire Redcap. As befitting the only organized and regulated race of its type in the world, the rules are strict: birds must begin the race with both feet on the ground, and no assistance from the handler – such as attempting to gain a few precious yards by means of an air-borne launch – is allowed. Any inducement in the way of laying a trail of food along the 66ft (20m) track is also frowned upon and could well result in immediate disqualification. Sometimes the race is a very slow affair, in which case the winner is determined after about three minutes by the hen that is the nearest to the finishing line – it is not unknown for contestants to stop halfway along the track and turn around to go back to the starting point.

There can be between 20 and 30 hens taking part and although most handlers are local, occasionally entrants have come from as far away as Chicago and Gibraltar, the latter borrowing

Riddles
In addition to the Hen Race, Bonsall boasts an unusual guided tour every August bank holiday Monday. Meeting at 11am, at The Barley Mow, the landlord shows walkers the 'dog that lives in a tree', 'people who have not been to bed for 65 years' and the 'stable where Cromwell hid his horses'!

birds from the pub in order to compete. Race trainers have until 1.30pm on the day to enter their birds; racing begins at 2pm; and the organizers aim to finish the championships by about 4pm when the Kimberley Classic Trophy (a large wooden running chicken) is presented to the winning owner. There are also prizes for runners-up, deportment, appearance and colour. Generally, a duplicate of each novelty prize is kept on show at The Barley Mow.

Healthy Living

The Hen Race is always a popular event with spectators, TV crews and reporters. The latter make much of the fact that Bonsall, a former lead-mining village perched on the Derbyshire Peaks and only a few miles from the Heights of Abraham near Matlock, is supposedly the healthiest village in England – a claim made as a result of the long lifespan of its inhabitants who, to walk from one end of the village to the other, need to either climb or descend some 492ft (150m).

Puck Fair

Killorglin, Co Kerry, Ireland (10–12 August)

There is occasionally some argument as to whether the Oul' Lammas Fair at Ballycastle (see page 147) is older than the Puck Fair, but there can be no doubt that the latter is by far Ireland's quirkiest festival. Where else would it possible to see a goat crowned king and elevated to a high stage so that he can oversee three days of music, revelry and raucous celebration?

As is often the case, the reason behind the custom is obscure, but two of the most commonly held theories concern Oliver Cromwell's troops and a man named Blennerhassett.

Goat Alert

Apparently, while Cromwell's soldiers were rampaging around the nearby Shanara and Kilgobnet areas they disturbed a herd of wild goats, which headed for the higher, and presumably safer, mountain slopes: all that is bar the billy (known in Ireland as a puck), who ran towards the settlement of Killorglin. Alerted by the arrival of the goat, which was obviously distressed and exhausted, the villagers realized that they wcre in imminent danger and took steps to protect both themselves and their property, thereby saving themselves

> ### Just a Name
> As well as being known as a puck, a male goat or billy was also known by the name of 'kilorglin' in Ireland. Could the real origin of the Puck Fair simply be that the settlement of Cill Orglain eventually became known as Killorglin and that it was appropriate to name the annual fair after the town?

from the Roundheads' onslaught. Ever grateful for the early warning, the town decided that a celebration should be held every year in honour of the billy goat.

Tax Collecting

For whatever reason it seems that a fair of some description has been held at Killorglin for at least 350 years. A second theory as to how it acquired the 'Puck' moniker has to do with nothing more fanciful than money. Before 1808 all livestock fairs were subject to a levy or toll, but at around that time an Act of Parliament decreed that should the Lord Lieutenant of Dublin wish to do so, he could make such demands for money unlawful. Mr Harman Blennerhassett – as a local landlord and Killorglin's collector of taxes – was understandably upset by the potential loss of revenue and employed the services of a local barrister, Daniel O'Connell, to see if there was a loop-hole in the decree that would allow him to continue collecting money from the people who attended the annual August live-stock fair. In the manner of a modern-day 'no-win, no fee' firm

Mind Your Language
The Puck Fair is one place where you might just still hear the true Irish language being spoken – it was once used throughout the whole island, but has progressively been driven westwards. Ironically, it was Irish invaders landing in Scotland that evolved the Gaelic language still spoken in the Scottish Highlands and Islands – resulting in the fact that a derivation of traditional Irish is more likely to be heard there than it is in its native country.

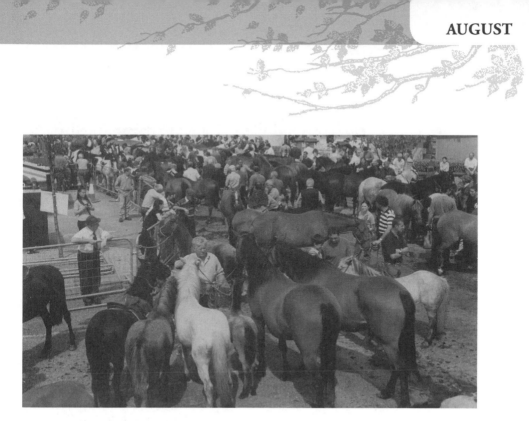

People and livestock at the Puck Fair

of solicitors, O'Connell managed to successfully claim that goats were not included in the Act and so if the livestock fair changed its name to a goat fair, Mr Blennerhassett would remain legally entitled to levy a toll to swell the town's coffers. To prove that it was, in fact, primarily a goat fair, not only was it advertised as such, but a goat was placed on a corralled stage as further evidence.

The Burryman

Every year the town of South Queensferry hosts the ritual of the Burryman, which has become an important part of the Ferry Fair despite the fact that the Burryman pre-dates the fair by many years – the fair itself began in 1687 and was originally held on St James' Day (25 July). Opinion is divided as to the origin of the name, some saying that Burry is a corruption of burgh, the Scottish name for a borough, while others believe that it is simply to do with the figure's covering of burrs.

Here Comes the Burryman

Whatever the root of his name, the Burryman is a strange creature almost guaranteed to send small children scuttling behind the nearest pair of parental legs when he appears on the streets of South Queensferry on the second Friday in August.

Carrying two flower-covered sticks, wearing a garlanded head-dress and covered from head to toe with literally hundreds of wild burdock burrs, the Burryman makes his debut in the morning, He is accompanied by two assistants who help him in his nine-mile (14km) trek around the town collecting money and dispensing good luck. The route varies, taking in both old and new parts of the town. Having successfully negotiated the crowds (at a rate of about one mile an hour), the Burryman arrives at The Hawes Inn where he officially opens the Ferry Fair sometime around 6pm.

Nowadays the person inside the costume is a native of Queensferry elected by the Ferry Fair committee, but who first donned the costume or what event he was portraying is open to speculation. In 1908, Isabel A Dickson wrote:

"The whole festival, Burryman and Fair together, is supposed to commemorate the great event of the crossing of the Firth of Forth and landing at South Queensferry by Margaret, wife of Malcolm Canmore. It is once clear that whatever may be true of the Fair, the Burryman procession belongs to a stage of belief much older than Queen Margaret (11th century). I would therefore suggest that the ceremony of the Burryman is a relic of an earlier propitiatory harvest rite."

It seems that most concur with Dickson's theory. The tradition is thought to be a survival of ancient nature worship, a representation of the god of harvest and an expression of hope for a bountiful yield but, like the Earl of Rone (see page 97), there is a strong possibility that the Burryman was nothing more than a scapegoat intended to collect and carry the sins of the town's inhabitants before being thrown into the sea or, like the effigy in Burning the Bartle (see page 143), burned. His origins may also be associated with the area's fishing industry – being an appeasement to the various sea-gods, who, it was believed, could either enhance or detract from the fishing harvest.

The unusual figure of the Burryman

Scarecrow Festival

Kettlewell, Yorkshire (a nine-day event usually running from the second Saturday in August to the following Sunday)

Kettlewell's annual Scarecrow Festival began in 1994 as a fundraising event for the local school and its rural catchment area in Upper Wharfedale. The enthusiastic response of parents and residents led to over a hundred scarecrows appearing in gardens, open spaces, churches, hidden corners and at house windows. So successful has the event been that it now attracts thousands of visitors over a nine-day period and other scarecrow festivals can now be found throughout the country (see right).

The Weird and the Wonderful

Each year, the imagination of local residents becomes more febrile. The scarecrows take the form of strange beings dressed as local well-known dignitaries, window cleaners, nuns and policemen. Ideas are also spawned by popular television programmes of the time, or include clever plays on

> ### Straw Figures
> Straw figures have been used throughout history to appease harvest gods and spirits (a corn dolly was believed to keep the corn spirit alive until the following spring). One tradition once found throughout Orkney at harvest time was the manufacture of a 'dog' from the last of the straw to be cut. This straw dog was known as the 'bikko' – a name derived from the Old Norse word bikkja, meaning bitch – and lifted to a prominent position in the stackyard, or on to one of the farm buildings belonging to the farmer who was last to finish his harvest. By the time the tradition came to be recorded the receipt of a bikko was regarded as the ultimate insult. Elsewhere in the country Jack O' Straw was, according to Webster's Dictionary, 'an effigy stuffed with straw; a man of straw; a man without property, worth or influence' – so he too ranks quite highly in the insult stakes.

words, such as a group of 'cereal' killers or a platoon of harvest scarecrows led by an army 'kernel'.

At Thornton Hough some years ago a basic wooden cross entitled Scarecrow on Holiday may be the cleverest, most effective and certainly the simplest idea yet. At one time Thornton Hough also held the world record for the most scarecrows in one place, but unfortunately lost the honour to a village in Portugal shortly afterwards.

Kettlewell, along with the other villages, produces a trail map plotting all the scarecrows in the locality.

Other Scarecrow Festivals
Also worth visiting are:
Wray, Lune Valley, Lancashire (late April–early May)
Urchfont, Wiltshire (early May)
Bassenthwaite, Cumbria (June)
Thornton Hough, Wirrel, Cheshire (June–July)
Langwathby, Cumbria (July)

Characters from The Wizard of Oz *in straw at the Kettlewell Festival*

Marhamchurch Revels

The Cornish Saint Morwenna apparently founded the village of Marhamchurch in a very unusual fashion. Not for her architects, a gang of tea-swilling builders and a battle with the local planning authorities: instead, in order to get the construction of the village church under way, the lady went off to the beach to carry back the necessary materials piece by piece herself. During one of these trips she dropped a rock and a water spring erupted from the indentation in the ground. Seemingly unaffected by this minor miracle, Morwenna picked up the rock and placed it as the cornerstone of her church.

Although Morwenna's feast day was 5 July, the inhabitants of Marhamchurch saw fit to celebrate the founding of their village in August, when today's revels begin outside the church.

A person representing Father Time (whose identity is not supposed to be known) crowns the Queen of the Revel (a local schoolgirl) who has been previously elected by her peers. The Queen then rides a white horse and leads a procession to the Revel Grounds where there are competitions, sideshows and bouts of Cornish wrestling.

Cornish Wrestling

The origins of Cornish wrestling are lost in prehistory, but it was certainly flourishing as an organized sport in Britain by Roman times. The main difference between Cornish and Cumberland wrestling, which is probably just as old, is the method of holding. In the Cornish style the contestants stand apart at the beginning of the bout, not grabbing hold of each other until the match begins. In Cumberland wrestling, the competitors begin with hands clasped behind each other's backs – one arm over the shoulder and one under – and this hold is maintained until a throw is achieved.

Rose of Tralee Festival

Tralee, Co Kerry, Ireland (a five-day event usually running from the third Thursday in August until the following Monday)

This international competition has its origins in a 19th-century Irish ballad that recounts the story of a local woman known because of her beauty as the Rose of Tralee. William Pembroke Mulchinock wrote the song after his affair with Mary O'Connor, a maid employed by his parents. There are several different versions of this tale, but the essence of the story is the timeless one of a hopeless love between two lovers from different social and religious backgrounds. Furthermore, Mulchinock apparently had to leave Ireland in a hurry and on his return found that his 'Rose' had died at the tragically young age of 29.

Beauty Contest
The festival, first held in 1959, came about as a way of drawing more visitors to the town during the annual Tralee horse-racing meeting. Irish communities from around the world, together with towns from all over Ireland, select a young woman aged between 18 and 25 to represent them at the contest: the winning 'Rose' being the one thought best to match the attributes of the girl in the song.

Rush-Cart Ceremony

The rush-cart ceremony at Saddleworth (revived in the mid-1970s) is a particularly old one and marks the weekend of the Saddleworth Wakes, when mills and factories had their annual week's holiday. In days gone by it was not uncommon for six or seven carts to be dragged to the door of the parish church. Great skill was involved in their construction and it was a matter of pride that the 15ft-high (5m) cart survived its journey intact. In wet years it was not unusual for the cart to be built in the comparative warmth of a barn – only to find that it was higher than the entrance.

The reeds (1,200–1,500 bundles) are collected from the moors about three weeks before the event and elaborately built on to the cart in the week prior to the ceremony. A jockey, picked from the Saddleworth

The rush-cart on its journey to the parish church

Morris men, rides the cart as Morris and mumming groups from the area pull it around the villages on the Saturday.

On Sunday morning the cart is pulled up the steep hill to the church for a service where it is blessed. A display from all the Morris sides follows outside the church.

Additional attractions over the weekend include competitions for wrestling, clog-stepping and 'gurning' (see page 156), and there is music in the pubs on both the Saturday and Sunday nights.

> *Horse Power*
> *At one time the best horses in the village pulled the cart and it would have been an honour to have your animal selected for the task. Morris dancers preceded them and the local youngsters walked beside the cart carrying garlands, which were hung in the church once the replacement rushes had been laid.*

Burning the Bartle

West Witton, North Yorkshire (Saturday nearest 24 August)

Bartle, a large guy-like effigy – usually more than life-size – is carried through the village amid boisterous chanting about 'his' eventual fate before being taken to Grassgill End where he is stabbed and set on fire.

Mystery Man

So who or what was Bartle to warrant such a dire fate? Legend has it that he may have been a local thief who was burned at the stake. Or he might have been a King Herod-type Norseman who, somewhat dismayed to find that his best pig had gone missing, had all the first-born sons brought to him with the promise that unless someone owned up to the pig's whereabouts he would kill them off one by one.

The original Bartle might have been a local abbot, a sort of early conscientious objector who tried unsuccessfully to avoid participating in a march to London organized in protest against the Reformation.

More probably, however, the name is derived from St Bartholomew: a conclusion given more credence by the fact that the Burning the Bartle ceremony is always held on the Saturday nearest to the 24th of the month – St Bartholomew's Day. When Henry VIII set about the dissolution of the monasteries and the removal of all church treasures, the parishioners of West Witton are thought to have tried hiding their statue of Bartholomew but were caught in the act by the king's soldiers who captured it from them at Grassgill End. The event is chronicled in the chant still very much a part of the Bartle celebrations:

> "*At Penhill Crags he tore his rags,*
> *At Hunter's Thorn he blew his horn,*
> *At Capplebank Stee he broke his knee*
> *At Grassgill Beck he broke his neck,*
> *At Waddam's End he couldn't fend*
> *At Grassgill End he met his end.*"

Like many other customs happening around this time of year, Burning the Bartle may well have been adapted from a sacrificial harvest ceremony.

BANK AND PUBLIC HOLIDAYS

A whole host of country customs take place around the August bank holiday period but this has more to do with the convenience of a long weekend rather than anything else.

Bank holidays were first introduced by the Bank Holidays Act of 1871, which designated four holidays in England, Wales and Northern Ireland, and five in Scotland. In England, Wales and Northern Ireland, both Christmas Day and Good Friday were already traditional 'common law' holidays and therefore did not need to be included in the Act.

Today's Bank and Public Holidays

England, Wales and Northern Ireland
New Year's Day (1 January)
Good Friday (variable)
Easter Monday (variable)
May Day or Early May Bank Holiday
    (first Monday in May)
Spring Bank Holiday or Whit Monday
    (last Monday in May)
Summer Bank Holiday
    (last Monday in August)
Christmas Day (25 December)
Boxing Day (26 December)

In Northern Ireland only
St Patrick's Day (17 March)

12 July (Anniversary of the Battle
    of the Boyne in 1690)

Scotland
New Year's Day (1 January)
New Year (2 January)
Good Friday (variable)
May Day or Early May Bank Holiday
    (first Monday in May)
Spring Bank Holiday or Whit Monday
    (last Monday in May)
Summer Bank Holiday
    (first Monday in August)
Christmas Day (25 December)
Boxing Day (26 December)

The 1871 Act was repealed 100 years later and its provisions incorporated into the Banking and Financial Dealings Act 1971, under which the following changes were introduced. Whit Monday in England, Wales and Northern Ireland (which could fall anywhere between 11 May and 14 June) was formally replaced by a fixed spring holiday on the last Monday in May. The last Monday in August was formally made a bank holiday in place of the first Monday in August in England, Wales and Northern Ireland. In Scotland, 2 January was created an additional bank holiday. New Year's Day became an additional bank holiday in England, Wales and Northern Ireland, and Boxing Day became an additional bank holiday in Scotland.

The first Monday in May in England, Wales and Northern Ireland, and the last Monday in May in Scotland, became additional bank holidays.

Changing Times

Nineteenth-century legislation introduced several other changes to people's working lives. For example, the 1833 Factory Act regulated the hours of women and teenagers, reducing their working week to 60 hours. Combined with the coming of the railways, it meant that for the first time ever suburban families could go away on holiday and take advantage of the late August weather – there were no such opportunities for rural families of course, as they were in the middle of their busy harvest. Prior to this period, holidays were entirely synonymous with religious festivals, rather than the rest and recreation with which we tend to associate them today.

Oul' Lammas Fair

The Lammas Fair at Ballycastle originated in the 17th century, most probably as a sheep market, and is famed as Ireland's oldest festival. It is always held over the summer bank holiday Monday and Tuesday. Today you are not restricted to shopping for sheep, as it's possible to buy anything from CDs to cattle; hats to horses; and frilly knickers to fancy food from the one hundred or so stalls and vending locations on site. Don't forget to try Dulce, a type of edible seaweed, and Yellowman, a delicious yellow toffee (see page 148).

Lammas

Although the Ballycastle Lammas fair is held at the end of August, Lammas Day (a derivative of 'Loaf-mass' Day) is actually 1 August – the date on which harvesting began. It was customary to take a loaf of bread made from the first sheaf of corn to church and have it blessed. In many parts of Britain tenants were also bound to give a sheaf of harvested wheat to their landlords, in addition to which, Lammas, being a Celtic quarter day, was a time when monetary rents were due and contracts negotiated.

In medieval times Lammas was known as the Gule of August, the word 'gule' possibly being an Anglicization of gwyl, the Welsh word for feast. Even before this, in pagan times there were feasts and fairs held in commemoration of Lugh, a god associated with the festival of Lunasdal. Lammas is also called the 'feast of the first fruits' and, in Richmond, North Yorkshire, the Ceremony of the First Fruits is still carried out each year.

DULSE AND YELLOWMAN

Dulse (*Palmaria palmate*) is a type of seaweed that grows along the northern coasts of the Atlantic. In Northern Ireland it is a well-known snack food. Traditionally, the seaweed is picked by hand at low tide through August and September and left out in the sun to dry before being either eaten as it is or ground to flakes or powder. It can also be pan-fried or baked in the oven covered with cheese. Dulse has always been a popular treat at Oul' Lammas Fair in Ballycastle (see page 147).

YELLOWMAN

Another delicacy found at the Lammas Fair is Yellowman, a type of honeycombed sticky toffee. To make it, you need:

1lb (½kg)/1½ cups of golden syrup
8oz (250g)/1 cup of brown sugar
A heaped tablespoon of butter
Two tablespoons of vinegar
One level tablespoon of baking powder

Using a large saucepan, slowly melt together all the ingredients (except the baking powder) and boil the mixture until a drop placed in cold water will immediately harden. Stir in the baking powder, at which point the toffee will foam up. Pour the concoction on to a greased surface and when it has cooled sufficiently fold the edges towards the centre and pull repeatedly until the toffee is a pale yellow colour, after which it should be left in a shallow tray to harden.

Crying the Neck

Madron, Penzance, Cornwall (first Friday in September)

Whereas the bigger Crying the Neck celebrations at Helston take place on the last Friday in August, thanks for the harvest are given at Madron a week later, at 6.30pm. At one time this particular harvest custom – where a sheaf of freshly scythed corn is woven into a corn dolly and hung in the church until the following year's harvest – was celebrated throughout Britain, but nowadays thrives only in Devon and Cornwall. Originally, the corn dolly would have been ploughed back into the soil the following spring – the theory being that the harvest spirit will live in the last sheaf to be cut and bring good fortune to the next year's farming operations.

Cornish Fare
At Madron, a church service and a simple supper of Cornish pasties (what else?), saffron buns and heavy cake follows the Crying the Neck ceremony. Heavy cake was traditionally taken by fishermen as part of their packed lunch and is said to get its name from the word 'hevva' – the cry of the fishermen's look-out man upon seeing a shoal of pilchards.

Cock in Britches

The Cock in Britches Cornish dance is thought to have originated as part of the Crying the Neck ritual, beginning as it does, with the words 'I ave'm, I ave'm, I ave'm! What ave ee, what ave ee, what ave ee? A neck, a neck, a neck' – which is similar to the chant used by the farm labourers as they cut the last sheaf of corn (neck); 'We ha' neck! We ha' neck! Hurrah, Hurrah! Hurrah!' The Cornish for this neck of corn is *Pedn Yar*, or *Pen Yar*, which literally means a chicken's head, and it therefore seems likely that the dance was part of a fertility rite performed to ensure next year's harvest by re-enacting the tasks associated with growing and reaping the corn.

Cock in Britches alludes to the fact that if you do not keep the weeds down they will handicap the corn in much the same way as a winning fighting cock was handicapped with a special hobble (britches) in order to even the odds in the cock-pit.

Babies, Girls, Maidens

In some northern areas, a corn dolly was known as a Kern Baby and although 'kern' is probably a corruption of the word corn, it may have originated from the Icelandic Kirna *– the feast of Harvest Home – a celebration where master and servants sat at the same table and spent the evening eating, drinking and dancing.*

In Kent, the custom took the form of the Ivy Girl – a figure made into a rough human shape with the best corn and adorned with paper trimmings cut to resemble a lace cap, ruffles and handkerchiefs, while in Scotland it was usual to made a figure known as the Maiden, which was dressed up in ribbons and brought to the Harvest Supper accompanied by the music of fiddles and bagpipes.

A corn dolly is held aloft at the Crying the Neck celebrations

Braemar Gathering

Braemar, Scotland (first weekend in September)

Although many Highland Games are held in Scotland throughout August and September, the Braemar Gathering is undoubtedly the best known, due mainly to the fact that it has long been attended by members of the Royal Family while holidaying at nearby Balmoral.

Traditional games of agility and strength have been practised in the Highlands for many generations and the origins of Braemar are said to go back to the 11th century. At this time King Malcolm III gave a prize to the winner of a race to the top of Craig Choinnich, but it was not until the 1820s that they were formalized and 'gatherings' were created. Queen Victoria was the first modern monarch to attend Braemar in 1848.

Tossing and Throwing

Scottish athletic competitions such as those held at Braemar tend to split into two categories: the Scottish Highland, or 'heavy' competitions, and traditional Celtic sporting events. Generally if the word 'toss' is included, it is a test of getting an object as high as possible, whereas those with 'throw' in their title normally require something to be propelled the longest possible distance. The most famous of these events must surely be Tossing the Caber, but other tests of skill, strength and endurance can be

The Wright Stuff

One of the early organizers of the Games was the Braemar Wright Society, which was a kind of insurance company. Wheelwrights and their ilk could join the society on payment of ten shillings and a subscription of a shilling a quarter. In return, they or their widow's would receive a pension of sorts and, in some cases; payment would be made in the event of a member being unable to work as a result of sickness or work-related injuries.

found at most Highland Games: these include the Sheaf Toss, Hammer Throwing and the Farmer's Walk (in which the athlete picks up two weights and walks for as long as he can around a series of pylons).

Traditional Celtic sports originated many centuries ago and were first practised by clansmen and soldiers using whatever items they had at their disposal, such as stones and weapons. The battle-axes used in modern competitions, for example, are frequently replicas of the type issued to the Fraser Highlanders. The axe is light enough to be used with one hand and yet heavy enough to dent or puncture armour. Fortunately for to-day's contestants, the axes are thrown at targets rather than at each other.

Unsurprising, kilts feature prominently at the Braemar Gathering and are worn by competitors and spectators alike. For the athletes, the weight of the kilt adds an additional challenge in events such as the running of the Kilted Mile – a Scottish version of a traditional track event.

As well as Scottish dancing, piping and drumming, some gatherings may also include a kilted golf tournament, fly-casting competitions, sheep-dog trials, harp playing, whisky tasting and even events in which female judges (often blindfolded) are asked to rate, by feel, the portion of the male leg that is exposed between the bottom edge of the kilt and the top of the stocking, or hose.

Different Rules

An event unique to this particular gathering is the Braemar Stone, which is similar to the normal Stone Throw (where a rounded stone, called a clachneart, *is used) except that, unlike the general competition where contestants can gain extra impetus to their throw by spinning around or 'gliding', the Braemar version does not permit any such movements.*

Abbots Bromley Horn Dance

Abbots Bromley, Staffordshire (first Monday after the first Sunday after 4 September. If the 4th is a Sunday, the event is held a week later on 12 September)

One of the best known and almost certainly one of the oldest of Britain's country customs, the Abbots Bromley Horn Dance is thought to date back as far as the Stone Age. Six men (known as Deermen) carrying heavy reindeer antlers and accompanied by a musician playing an accordion, a Hobby Horse, a transvestite, a Fool and two boys (one with a triangle, the other with a crossbow) – all the ingredients of a good day out! – begin the festivities outside the Vicarage at 8am. By late evening, having danced and indulged in mock battles among themselves throughout the village and at Blithfield Hall (this the only day of the year it is open to the public) and at many outlying farms and houses, it is reckoned that the Deermen and their entourage will have covered between 10 and 20 miles (6 and 14km) in their massive luck-bringing marathon.

An Unlikely Theory
One school of thought suggests the Horn Dance is, in fact, a more recent phenomenon and began about 1,000 years ago as an assertion of local forestry rights. However, although the horns used in today's ceremony are known to date from around that time, the fact that the Norman aristocracy guarded their hunting forests so intensely that anyone found poaching lost either a hand or an eye for a first offence and his life for a second, it seems unlikely that anyone would be foolish enough to boast of their poaching success by prancing around the village with a brace of antlers strapped to his head!

The Origins of the Dance

Most of the Deermen have long-standing family connections with the dance stretching back over several generations. They carry their horns fixed to a carved wooden stag's head, thereby clearly representing the hunted rather than the hunters. The 'transvestite', in reality a big man obviously dressed as a woman, is known as Maid Marion even though the dance predates the legends of Robin Hood. He carries a ladle to collect money from passers-by. The Fool dances complete with a pig's bladder tied to a stick and, at certain points during the day, the boy bowman makes as if to let loose an arrow at the dancing Deermen. This ritual is

The dancing Deermen of the Abbots Bromley Horn Dance

carried out in the hope of ensuring a good hunt and, judging from paintings discovered in the caves at Lascaux in France with similar images, is believed to date back over 20,000 years ago. The Abbots Bromley Horn Dance may therefore have begun either because of the belief that imitating a hunt gives the hunters magical powers, or, common to theories held by primitive peoples all over the world, that wearing the skin and antlers of the proposed quarry gives the hunter protection from danger.

Whatever the mysteries surrounding the Horn Dance itself, there are no such problems in identifying the origins of the costumes. Until the early 1860s the participants dressed in their own clothes, but then the two daughters of the local vicar, a certain Reverend Lowe, decided to design outfits for the entourage, taking as their inspiration costumes that were shown in their illustrated book of Shakespeare. Now the clothes are as much a part of the tradition as the reindeer horns.

Horns Dilemma

Perhaps the most mysterious part of the custom is the fact that the horns are those of reindeer rather than of the red or fallow deer that might have been found in English woodland. Where did the horns in use today come from? There were certainly no reindeer in England 1,000 years ago. If the horns originated from a Scandinavian country, did the Horn Dance have its source there too? Throughout the year the horns can be seen in a side-chapel at St Nicholas' Church.

Egremont Crab Fair and Gurning Championships

The Egremont Crab Fair was first held in 1267, when King Henry III granted a royal charter for a weekly Wednesday market and an annual fair to be held on 7, 8 and 9 September. As time progressed the fair was reduced to a one-day event held on 19 September, and in 1889 the date of the fair was changed again to 18 September. Nowadays, with many people working a five-day week, it has become traditional to hold the fair on the third Saturday in September.

Little is known about the events of the Crab Fair before the 19th century. Cock fighting and bull baiting were popular attractions and continued at the fair when they were prohibited by law. Another crowd-pleaser was the 'greasy pole', which was over 30ft (9m) high and greased with lard. The objective was to climb to the top and retrieve the prize – originally a hat, which the winner wore as he paraded around the town. In 1852 the prize became a side of mutton, which, if not won by the end of the day, was cut up and divided among the poor. The tradition continues to this day and in addition to the main prize, ribbons, which can be grabbed from lower levels and exchanged for gifts, are now attached to the pole.

Further sports always commenced after the 'scattering of apples' at midday – now known as the Parade of the Apple Cart. It is not known exactly when this spectacle originated, but it is thought that it was a celebration of the completion of the harvest when labourers gathered crab apples and other wild fruits to help pay their dues to the lord of the manor. Nowadays the sour crab apples have been replaced by sweeter eating varieties, which are thrown into the crowd from the back of a cart or wagon.

Races Galore

Crab Fair events get off to a flying start on Friday evening when fancy dress wheelbarrow races are held on Main Street. In the adult race each competitor is required to drink half a pint of beer at every public house along the route. The children's race follows the same route, but the beer is replaced by soft drinks.

The next morning a large group of riders on horseback parade around the streets of Egremont in a tradition known as Riding the Fair, while groups of runners participate in fell racing. More races are held on the sports field along with traditional Cumberland and Westmorland wrestling, dog and ferret shows, poultry and pigeon shows, a gymkhana, a fly-casting competition and many side stalls. Cumberland hound trailing, where the hounds follow a trail of aniseed across the fields and fells surrounding Egremont, is also a popular spectator sport. The rest of the day's amusements include the singing of hunting songs and, of course, the World Gurning Championship.

Pulling Faces

For those who may not be aware, gurning is the art of pulling grotesque faces. The dictionary definition of the word gurn is 'to snarl like a dog, look savage, distort the countenance', and some of the best contestants manage to do all three. The championships are, as the title suggests, attended by competitors from all over the world and begin with a junior competition, which is then followed by the ladies' before culminating with the world's best contorting their faces into seemingly impossible arrangements. It seems that mother may have been right when she used to say 'Stop pulling faces – one day the wind will blow and your face will stay like that.'

Hop Hoodening

Canterbury, Kent (early September)

Unlike similar ceremonies held elsewhere in the country (the double 'o' is used only in Canterbury), which are usually carried out at Christmas or Halloween, the hoodening event at Canterbury takes place in early September and celebrates the forthcoming hop-harvest. Like many other country customs, hodening has its origins in pagan fertility rites, protection from evil spirits and the hope of bringing good fortune.

The Hooden Horse, which forms a major part of the Canterbury festivities, usually takes the form of a man dressed in a stable-blanket or similar covering who carries a horse's head with reins attached to a pole. Other revellers, one of whom takes the part of Mad Mollie, lead the horse: Mollie carries a broom while the rest carry bells and other musical instruments. The head was sometimes made of wood, but more usually it was a real horse skull with hinged jaws that could be made to snap open and shut. Sometimes a lighted candle would be fixed in the head in much the same way as in a turnip lantern at Halloween (see page 176). According to Christina Hole in her book *British Folk Customs* (Book Club Associates 1976):

> "… *accompanied by a band of young men, the man-horse walked at night through the dark streets and lanes, with a crouching gait to make him look like a four-footed beast … Nervous people were often alarmed by the sudden appearance of this weird-looking creature on their doorsteps; … one woman, coming face to face with him without warning, was so terrified that she died of fright.*"

Never will it ever be more appropriate to tell your friends and colleagues to stop 'horsing' around!

Widecombe Fair

The fair at Widecombe began in the early 1850s as a livestock market and has been held in one form or another every year since – with a break during World War II and in 2001 due to the foot-and-mouth outbreak. It was during the war break, when farmers had to find an alternative place to buy and sell their animals, that the fair became more of a show. Today there are cattle, sheep and Dartmoor pony classes, as well as terrier races, a family dog show, displays of vintage vehicles and machinery, a gymkhana, maypole dancing, rural crafts, fancy dress competitions, bale-tossing contests and a tug-of-war.

Uncle Tom Cobley and All

The well-known folk song *Widecombe Fair*, which tells the story of Uncle Tom Cobley and the sad fate of the old grey mare he and his friends borrowed from Tom Pearce, can be traced back to well before 1850. The words and tune vary in different parts of the country, although the story and characters remain constant. Incidentally, the original Tom Cobley would have had no need to hitch a lift on Tom Pearce's unfortunate beast as he was a well-to-do farmer more than able to finance his own transport to the fair. He died in 1794 having lived to the age of 96 and is buried at Spreyton, just north of Dartmoor, where his grave can still be seen.

STRUAN MICHEIL

St Michael is the patron saint of fishermen in Scotland and in the Hebrides he was given the status of a pagan sea-god. There was feasting and dancing on St Michael's Eve (28 September) and a cake known locally as Struan Micheil was baked specially for the occasion. This was made from sheep's milk (sheep were considered to be sacred animals), eggs, butter and cereal, and its manufacture was normally the responsibility of the eldest daughter in the family – guided by her mother and assisted by her sisters. As she moistened the dough with the sheep's milk, it was customary for her to recite 'To the progeny and prosperity of this family, the mystery of Michael, protection of the Trinity'.

When the 'struan' was ready for baking, it was placed on a flat rock and covered by a lamb's skin, which was then positioned on the edge of an open fire made of rowan, oak and bramble. Each individual struan was meant to have certain significance and one may have been made for every member of the family. Sometimes local fruits or honey would be added and a cross marked on each cake. Once cooked, a piece would be broken off and thrown into the fire in the hope that it would appease the Devil, with the remainder being taken to church for a blessing on St Michael's Day. It would then be eaten as part of the day's main meal, along with the traditional dish of roast lamb.

Gathering St Michael's Carrots

On the afternoon of the Sunday preceding Michaelmas, women and girls in the Hebrides gather wild carrots. However, it's not sufficient to dig them up in any old way – a special ritual must be adhered to. Firstly, triangular holes are dug with a three-pronged fork; the holes represent St Michael's shield and the fork his trident. As the carrots are being dug up, the participants recite the following verse:

"Cleft, fruitful, fruitful, fruitful,
Joy of carrots surpassing on me
Michael the brave endowing me
Bride [St Brigid] the fair be aiding me."

Afterwards the carrots are tied together with red ribbon and given to any visitors who may happen to call on Michaelmas day. Any carrots with forked roots, especially those with three 'prongs', are thought to be especially lucky.

FAIRS

Although many fairs are traditionally held throughout the British Isles at all times of the year, it seems to be the months of September and October that contain the most. This is especially obvious around Michaelmas, a period that marked the end of harvest and a time when farmers could calculate how many animals they could afford to keep through the winter without running low on fodder. Livestock surplus to requirements would either have to be slaughtered and then smoked or salted to preserve the meat, or sold on at one of the many Michaelmas fairs.

HIRING FAIRS

In addition to livestock fairs, rural folk attended hiring fairs, which were particularly important for farm labourers looking for winter employment after the harvest. The hiring fair began in medieval times when the Statute of Labourers Act empowered local magistrates to fix the agricultural workers' rate of pay and to make those rates known at

the Sessions or Statute Fair, normally held at Martinmas, May Day or Michaelmas. By the time such rates had been abolished, the Statute Fair had become such a well-known place for country people to gather that it was a good venue for farmers to employ their workers and for workers to seek work. The name eventually changed to a hiring or mop fair and those seeking employment would stand in the town square carrying the tools of their

trade so would-be employers could identify them: a crook for a shepherd, a whip for a carter, a milking bucket for a dairymaid, and so on.

A contract of sorts would be made between the two parties and there was sometimes a primitive 'get-out' clause so that, should the agreement prove unsuitable, both employer and employee could try for a more successful placing at the 'runaway' mop fair held in the locality a few weeks later.

Goose Fairs

Michaelmas was one of the regular quarter days for paying rents and settling accounts. Often, since this was a time of the goose 'harvest', farmers would pay off their debts with a brace or more of young, spring-hatched geese. Goose fairs were traditionally held a few weeks later, to which birds would be driven from all parts of the country. In an effort to protect their feet from damage on the rough stone roads and tracks the geese had their feet dipped in warm tar, which would form a solid base. Of all the goose fairs, Nottingham and Tavistock are probably the most famous still in existence but they are now simply pleasure events entirely lacking in geese.

Horse Fairs

The Barnet Horse Fair is also still held every year and, unlike the goose fairs, where the only connection to livestock is in its name, there are still plenty of horses to be seen. The fair has been in existence for around 800 years and its close proximity to London has always made it a great event. Today the old fair ground is now a housing estate and the fair takes place on the first weekend in September at the 'new' site of Greengate stables. Other horse fairs held in September include Latter Lee in West Yorkshire.

The Hand of Friendship

Wherever people gathered at fairs, it was not long before tradesfolk turned up to show off their wares – it being far more economical to take products to a certain point rather than hawk them around the scattered hamlets on the off-chance of a sale. A fair had the advantage of concentrating potential buyers from miles around, as well as bringing together people who would not otherwise have met.

For many years the symbol of a large, often white, glove or a wooden hand was displayed at the entrance to fairs as a sign of friendship and free trade. At Barnstaple, for example, the fair opens when a large glove garlanded with flowers is suspended from a window at the Guildhall, while in the past, at Exeter's Lammas Fair, a stuffed glove was carried on a decorated pole in the opening procession, and during the summer and autumn fairs held at Chester a painted wooden hand used to be hung on the Church of St Peter.

WEATHER WARNINGS

October figures in numerous sayings and traditional rhymes to do with the weather. Here's one:

*"If ducks do slide at Hallow-tide,
At Christmas they do swim;
If ducks do swim at Hallow-tide,
At Christmas they will slide."*

Many weather predictions for the month seem to be based around birds: if, for example, fieldfares and redwings are seen during October, a hard winter is sure to follow. Tradition also has it that if a squirrel has a bushy tail, it indicates a cold snap (in reality, a bushy tail is an early-warning system to other squirrels). Likewise, a plethora of fruits such as blackberries (and don't forget to pick them in early October otherwise the witches will have spat on them) is said to indicate inclement weather ahead.

The moon also plays its part in predictions for this time of year:

*"Rain in October
Gives wind in December.
If the October moon comes without frost,
Expect no frost until the moon of November."*

A halo around the moon was generally considered to be a portent of bad weather and the eeriness of its appearance may have fuelled the superstitions and customs associated with Halloween.

Finally, for every fog in October, there will apparently be a snowfall in the winter.

British Lawn Mower Racing Grand Prix

On the first weekend of October, Wisborough Green, a traditional West Sussex village, becomes the venue for roaring, snorting, petrol-driven engines, each one of which hopes to cut the mustard – well, to be more accurate, the grass.

Like the World Coal Carrying Championships, the Nettle Eating Contest, the Scarecrow Festival, the Rose of Tralee Festival, Dwile Flonking and the World Conker Championships, the British Lawn Mower Racing Grand Prix is another tradition that began in the latter half of the 20th century but looks set to become a curious country custom of the future.

The sport was conceived in 1973 in The Cricketers Arms in Wisborough Green. A group of locals, along with Jim Gavin, an Irishman who had raced and rallied cars across the world, were downing their pints when they looked across the village green to see the green keeper mowing the cricket pitch. Gavin had become disillusioned with the increasing costs of motorsport and was keen to create a cheaper form of the event, easily accessible to all: the lawn mower suddenly seemed to be the answer.

Boys Toys Rule OK!

The first race meeting was held in a local farmer's field with about 80 entries. Nowadays as many as 250 competitors participate in the 12-date racing calendar, which begins in May and ends in October, incorporating the British Championship, the World Championships, the British Grand Prix and, most famous of all, the 12 Hour Endurance Race. There are several categories of mower, ranging from manually operated and hand-driven machines right through to the most up-to-date sit-on variety. Obviously, the rules alter depending on the class.

Old Man's Day

At 4pm on 2 October (unless the date falls on a weekend, in which case it moves to 10am), children with brooms start sweeping at the top of Fleece Lane. The ceremony marks a day in the 16th century when farmer Matthew Wall's coffin was dropped in the lane while on its way to the churchyard. The jolt awoke the 'corpse' and he lived on for several years. Understandably pleased at this turn of events, Matthew left a request in his will that after he died the church bells be rung every year on 2 October to mark the anniversary of his escape and that a poor man be paid to sweep the street between his house and the church gate.

Lost in the Dark Bells

Someone else who had cause to thank his good fortune was Hampshire man William Davis. One dark and foggy night while riding home on his horse he became hopelessly disorientated but hadn't the sense to slow down from a gallop. Hearing the bells of Twyford church ringing out from a totally unexpected direction, he pulled his horse up sharply and in doing so prevented them both from falling to their certain death over the edge of a quarry. So grateful was he to the bells that, like Mr Wall (see above), Davis left money in his will for them to be rung every year on 7 October, thus beginning the Lost in the Dark Bells tradition.

World Conker Championships

Every year in Aston modern-day gladiators fight for glory armed with nothing more than a nut and short piece of string. Not only do great oaks from little acorns grow, but so too it seems does the lowly chestnut fruit and the World Conker Championships. Things apparently started in a very small way back in 1965 when a group of regulars at the local pub were thwarted by bad weather in their attempt to organize a fishing expedition. Someone suggested that they play conkers instead and the rest, as they say, is history.

Competitors battle it out at the World Conker Championships

Strikes and Strings

Each player has a conker threaded on a piece of knotted string and players take turns at hitting their opponent's conker. The conker to be hit first should hang perfectly still from the string, which is best wrapped round the player's hand. It must be held at the height your opponent chooses. Your opponent, the striker, takes his conker in the other hand and draws it back for the strike. Releasing the conker, he swings it down by the string held in the other hand. If he misses, he is allowed up to two further goes. If the strings tangle, the first player to call 'strings' gets an extra shot. Players take alternate hits at their opponent's conker and the game is won when one conker is destroyed. In some tournaments a winning conker can then go on with an enhanced score to do battle with other conkers. At the World Championships, however, the winner is decided by a knockout system.

On the Day!
The competitors play on eight small stages on the village green and go through a number of rounds until a winner emerges, who is then led to the Conker Throne to be crowned with conkers. There are separate competitions for men, ladies and juniors. The events begin at 10am and, aside from the tension, nail-biting and bruised knuckles associated with the tournament, there are Morris dancing displays and other traditional customs to look forward to.

Moot Horn Curfew

Ripon, North Yorkshire (every day of the year)

Every night for over 1,000 years the city horn has been sounded in Ripon – four times in the market place and once outside the mayor's house – in a tradition that goes back to Anglo-Saxon times. Before the days of civic mayors, most towns had a Wakeman whose duty it was to keep law and order and to protect the townsfolk from harm. One of the ways of doing this was to impose a curfew between the hours of 9pm and sunrise. Any robbery or injury between these times could then be proven to have occurred as a result of negligence on the part of the Wakeman or his officers and the victim could claim compensation. The sounding of the horn was a signal that all good people should be at home and also that the Wakeman's watch had begun.

Even in those days it seems that it was impossible to get something for nothing and each household had to pay 2d for every outer door on their home as a kind of insurance premium.

Moot Horns

Several ancient towns have moot horns (cow horns made into instruments) included in their treasures. They were used in the Middle Ages to call citizens together in times of danger and were later used to summon members of the Assemblies of the Burroughs Mote – forerunners of today's town councils. It was also common for the horn to be associated with the city watch.

Horn Days

In addition to his nightly duties, it was the Wakeman's responsibility to blow his horn on each of the five Horn Days – Candlemas Day, at Rogan-tide, the Feast of St Wilfred in August, 12 October and 26 December (St Stephen's Day). Over the years these dates have altered slightly so that they now include Easter. When the city mayor replaced the office of Wakeman in 1604, it was decided to appoint an official Hornblower – a position that still exists today.

The horn blown each evening is not the original, although this is still in existence and is paraded on ceremonial occasions by Ripon's Sergeant-at-Mace.

Taking the Biscuit
Not content with its ancient daily horn-blowing ceremony, Ripon is also home to the Wilfred Procession held in honour of St Wilfred. As part of the 'Ripon1100' celebrations in 1986, the two events were commemorated and connected by the creation of a Mummers play (see December for more on 'Mumming'). The play is now performed each year during August, at the culmination of which, unique horn-shaped biscuits are distributed – thus supplying yet another new curious country custom.

Titchfield Carnival

Titchfield, Hampshire (first weekend of October half-term holiday – third/fourth week)

Many reasons are offered as to the origins of the first Tichfield Carnival, which is known to have been in existence since at least 1880. It may have come from a tradition of riotous celebrations connected with a defunct autumn fair, but the favourite story involves the burning of an effigy of a local anti-hero. Quite who this was is a mystery – the 3rd Earl of Southampton would be a likely candidate were it not for the fact that he died over 250 years before the first carnival took place.

No full description of the carnival comes to light until 1894, when the local newspaper records that people paraded round the town in costume with an effigy, a local drum band and torch bearers before adjourning to a field for a firework display. By 1898, topical tableaux were included in the celebrations, together with a trades' procession.

Over the years the idea of tableaux has continued, but they are only part of an event that has, on occasion, included scarecrows on horseback, gypsies and witches, children dressed as animals, shire horses pulling a brewery dray, wagonettes and tractors.

After the Bonfire Queen is crowned in the early afternoon the carnival begins with the first of two processions, the second being held in the evening prior to the lighting of the bonfire at around 9pm. Other attractions include fireworks, funfair, dancing and the competition (usually 'themed') for the best-decorated shops, houses, pubs and hotels.

Stow Gypsy Horse Fair

Stow-on-the-Wold, Gloucestershire
(Thursdays nearest 12 May and 24 October)

In 1476 the Abbot of Evesham obtained a charter for two sheep fairs to be held at Stow: the first on 12 May, the feast of St Philip and St James, the second on 24 October, the feast of St Edward the Confessor. As the importance of sheep declined in the Cotswolds, the fairs eventually became horse fairs, favoured by farmers, huntsmen, professional dealers and gypsies. Today the Stow fair is now one of the biggest gatherings of its kind in England, the horse-drawn caravans and colourful characters attracting photographers and artists, as well as the public.

Several other horse fairs exist throughout the British Isles; some, but not all, originated as a result of being granted a Charter by various monarchs.

Probably the other best-known horse fair still in existence is at Appleby-in-Westmorland, Cumbria and lasts a week. Held in early June, the exact dates are defined by the fact that the last day of trading is the second Wednesday of the month. Like Stow, it is famous for its picturesque atmosphere and as a gathering ground for travelling families – so much so that at Appleby, there can be almost 1,000 caravans (sadly most of which are now motor, rather than horse-drawn) parked on Gallows Hill where the fair has been held since circa 1750.

At any horse fair, it pays to have eyes in the back of your head: horse traders let nothing get in the way of showing off the paces of their animals to a prospective buyer and, difficult though it may be to believe, with the hustle and noise, it's not always possible to hear an on-coming horse (often harnessed to a cart) until you've been run over – I know, I was that man!

Oyster Feast

Colchester, Essex (last Friday in October)

The Oyster Feast, along with the ceremonial opening of the oyster season on 1 September, celebrates Colchester's long association with oyster fishing. Beginning with the Romans, the trade was put on a more official footing when King Richard I handed over the fisheries to the townspeople in 1186.

Originally the feast was held on 20 October – the date of the town's St Dennis Fair – but nowadays it takes place on the last Friday in October at the Moot Hall. At one time the citizens of the town would have paid for the feasting but today entry is by ticket. Councillors, guests and civic dignitaries have the first option, and 40 places are reserved for members of the public: tickets are allocated on a ballot system.

Supply and Demand

It is said that oysters were one of the main reasons for the Roman invasion of these shores. While this may be something of an exaggeration, we do know that the Romans enjoyed enormous quantities of British oysters and that the precious molluscs were exported in large quantities back to Italy. Once plentiful around the British coastline, native oysters were seriously over-harvested during the late 19th century and as a result have become the expensive luxury they are today. In years gone by, however, they were a staple diet of the poor.

Other Oyster Festivals

Less exclusive than Colchester, Whitstable in Kent also holds an annual oyster festival. This is open to the public and celebrated with oyster landings, an oyster tasting and a blessing of the fishing boats.

In Ireland the grandly named International Oyster Festival takes place in Galway during September: the main events are the Guinness Irish Oyster Opening Championship and the Guinness World Oyster Opening Championship – no prizes for guessing the name of the sponsors. Other events include the selection and crowning of the Oyster Pearl and a huge party.

In Anglesey, a four-day Oyster and Seafood Festival is held over either the first or second weekend in October.

Food of Love

Oysters are considered to be one of the world's classic aphrodisiacs. Legend has it that the great lover Casanova ate 50 raw oysters every morning. For the greatest potency, eat them raw, on the half shell. Although the reasons for attraction and desire are almost as much a mystery today as they were in ancient times, it is now known that the spur for sexual desire begins in the brain – in the hypothalamus, which also governs our appetites for food and drink.

When buying oysters, make sure that the shells are firmly shut. If any shells are open slightly, tap sharply. Any that do not close immediately should be discarded. Although best eaten on the day of purchase, oysters will keep for five to seven days if kept cool and are loosely covered with a damp cloth or seaweed in the bottom of the fridge, with the flat shell uppermost to retain the juices.

HALLOWEEN

Christians have always known 31 October as the Eve of All Hallows (Saints) Day, but it was also the last day of the year in the old Celtic calendar. The Druids celebrated it as *Samhain*, a word believed to be derived from *sain*, meaning 'summer' and *fuin*, meaning 'ending.'

Initially associated with witches and pagan festivals, Halloween now represents a curious divergence of custom in Christian terms; for while in Catholic countries the faithful still place flowers on the graves of the departed, the Protestant section of the community have always celebrated by having a good time.

TRADITIONS

There are many traditions connected to Halloween. In Scotland in particular it was celebrated with bonfires and 'guising' as children dressed up and went round neighbouring houses with 'tattie bogles' or 'neep' lanterns (candles inside turnips). Children in southern England who would take their carved pumpkins through the

Jack O'Lanterns

Despite its popularity throughout Britain and America, the use of Jack O' Lanterns stems from Irish folklore. Jack, a notorious drunkard and trickster, persuaded the Devil to climb a tree and trapped him there by carving an image of the cross in the bark of the trunk. A deal was made in which the Devil promised never to tempt Jack again.

After Jack died, his bad ways prevented him from entering Heaven and the Devil got even by denying him access to Purgatory. Out of kindness, Satan did, however, allow Jack a small ember to light his way through eternal darkness: the ember being placed in a hollowed-out turnip to keep it glowing longer.

streets singing Punky songs also carried out this tradition of Jack O'Lanterns, using pumpkins rather than turnips. Correctly, Punky Night is the fourth Thursday of October, but pumpkins are generally used nowadays in Halloween celebrations.

In Northern England, Halloween became known as Nut Crack Night and girls anxious to know the identity of their future husband would place two hazelnuts in the fire side by side and give them names. If the fire caused the nuts to fly and burst apart, the signs were bad; if they burned together, the omen was good. Alternatively, pulling a cabbage from the garden on this night is also supposed to determine the suitability or otherwise of a future partner: roots full of dirt indicate his or her prosperity while its taste – bitter or sweet – is said to equate to their temperament. Leave the stalk wedged over a door and the name of the first person to dislodge it is the name of who you'll marry.

Apples

Other Halloween customs include dunking for, or attempting to bite, apples hung from string with hands tied behind one's back – a custom that probably has its origins in the plight of Tantalus, a Greek god, who was hung from the Tree of Life but could not reach the fruit nor slake his thirst.

MAKING MISCHIEF

In Yorkshire, Mischief Night is 4 November, but elsewhere, children make mischief on Halloween and this tradition arises from the belief that witches are out en masse causing trouble wherever they see an opportunity.

Bells and bonfires were rung and lit to help the dead find their way back from Hell so that their souls might spend this night with their families.

Hop-Tu-Naa

Cregneash, Isle of Man (31 October)

In the Isle of Man, Halloween was known as Holland-tide Eve or Hop-Tu-Naa, a name believed to have the same origin as the Scottish Hogmanay. Marking the end of summer, it was a time for celebrating the completion of the harvest and everything being in readiness for the long dark winter ahead. Traditionally, the boys of the Isle of Man would go from house to house carrying turnips or cabbages on sticks and hope to be rewarded with apples, *bonnag* (a tea plate-sized fruit cake), herring and possibly some sweets and the odd penny in return for chanting:

"Hop-Tu-Naa – I met an old woman
Tra-la-laa – She was baking bonnags
Hop-Tu-Naa – I asked for a bit
Tra-la-laa – She gave me a bit, as big as my big toe.
Hop-Tu-Naa – She dipped it in milk
Tra-la-laa – She wrapped it in silk
Hop-Tu-Naa, Tra-la-laa
Jinny the Witch flew over the house
To catch a stick to lather the mouse
Hop-Tu-Naa, Tra-la-laa
If you don't give us something we'll run away
With the light of the moon."

The girls would stay at home in order to discover whom they were likely to marry: 'dumb' cake or *soddag valloo* (made from flour, eggs, water and suet) was baked and eaten in silence. One piece was eaten while walking backwards towards the bed, after which it was guaranteed that a future husband would appear in your dreams. Other ways of discovering the identity of a partner included eating a salted herring, eggs (shells and all) and soot.

Tar Barrel Racing

Ottery St Mary, Devon (5 November)

In these health and safety-conscious days it is amazing that the potentially dangerous practice of Tar Barrel Racing (or rolling) still exists – there has to be an element of madness in anyone voluntarily hoisting up a lit barrel on to their shoulders and careering off down the village street for no apparent reason. As yet, however, it appears that there are no immediate plans to ban the custom though it seems there are problems in gaining adequate insurance for the event.

The custom is thought to have originated in the 17th century as a way of cleansing the streets of evil spirits. Nowadays, each of the town's pubs sponsors a barrel and in the weeks preceding the event the barrels are soaked with tar. From about 4pm on 5 November things begin to hot up as each barrel is lit and carried or rolled up and down the streets until the flames and constant battering have totally destroyed them. Women and children start the proceedings with lighter barrels, then the men take over with bigger and heavier barrels – sometimes weighing as much as 66lbs (30kg). There is likely to be plenty of activity until well after midnight, not just in the streets but also around the gigantic 30ft (10m) bonfire.

Generation Game

Traditionally, generations of the same family take part and it is not unusual for one man to hand over his load to his brother, son, father or even grandfather.

Turning the Devil's Stone

At 8pm on 5 November, while the rest of the country is burning effigies of Guy Fawkes, Shebbear in Devon has its own unique celebration. A report in *The Times* on 4 November 1952 said:

"The pride of the village is the brown monolith – an arenaceous conglomerate stone – that reposes beneath an oak-tree outside the Norman church. On the evening of 5 November the bell-ringers unfailingly assemble in the belfry with a designedly clamorous and discordant peal, which is looked upon as a challenge to evil spirits. Accompanied by the Vicar the ringers then leave the church, arm themselves with crowbars, and surround the boulder. Shouting excitedly, as though to encourage one another, they then turn over the boulder."

So there you have it. The one-tonne lump of rock known as the Devil's Stone is what geologists know as a glacial erratic, i.e. a piece of rock that has been transported some distance by glacial action and therefore differs in type and size from the rocks in the area in which it is found.

One particular legend has it that the stone, quarried on the other side of the River Torridge, was intended as the foundation stone for a new church but the Devil rolled it to Shebbear. The villagers then rolled it back to where it belonged, and the Devil rolled it back again. This game could have continued forever if the villagers hadn't eventually trapped the Devil beneath the stone to keep him imprisoned there for all eternity – provided that the stone is turned once a year, otherwise disaster will fall upon the village and its residents.

BONFIRES

There are a great many country customs that concern themselves with fire in November but surprisingly few have anything to do with Guy Fawkes and his ill-fated plans to blow up the Houses of Parliament. The tar barrels of Ottery St Mary (see page 179) clear the streets of undesirable creatures from another world and Samhain is one of the four Celtic fire festivals marking the quarter points of the year, at each of which feasts are held and bonfires lit.

Fire has long been thought to possess purifying qualities, cleaning and rejuvenating both the land and its people. Animals would be brought into shelter from the winter weather but they were first driven between several bonfires in the hope that they would be freed of evil spirits – a rather inefficient form of disinfectant, one can only assume.

At other times of the year, the ritualistic lighting of fire to welcome the sun and the arrival of summer would ensure the fertility of the land and the people – the Celts leapt over Beltane fires and young men would circle the fire holding branches of rowan as a protection against evil.

Saint Walburga

Walpurgis Night, closely connected to May Day and most probably stemming from the pagan rite of Beltane, is celebrated with bonfires on 30 April or May Day. It is apparently named in honour of Saint Walburga, the patron saint of coughs, famine, plague and storms. Born in Wessex around 710, Walburga travelled with her uncle and brothers to Germany where she became Abbess of Heidenheim Kloster. There she was involved in healing many of the local people and was canonized by Pope Adrian II on 1 May 77AD, a few months after her death on 25 February. Whether it is merely a coincidence that the date of her canonization coincided with many pagan rituals celebrating the coming of new life and spring is uncertain, but it did at least mean that people had a double excuse to celebrate both events under Church law.

Bonfire Bonanzas

On the afternoon of 11 January, preparations for Burning the Clavie get underway at Burghead in Morayshire and are once again a protection against evil, as are the fire festivals on New Year's Eve (see page 214).

At Lewes in East Sussex torchlight processions of burning effigies, fireworks and rolling tar barrels make their way through the streets towards one of a number of raging bonfires commemorating the martyrdom of 17 local people burned at the stake in the reign of Mary Tudor.

Wroth Silver Ceremony

The Wroth Stone can be found at the top of Knightlow Hill on a mound that, some say, marks the resting place of the Danish warrior Colbran. The stone, worn and misshapen, measures about 30in (76cm) square at the top and has a deep rounded hollow in its centre.

The origins of the ceremony may well be pagan, given the connections with a white bull, the fact that each person paying the Wroth Silver has to walk three times around the stone and that it takes place as the sun rises. Another theory suggests that it may have arisen from the need to pay money to avoid military duties, but the most commonly held belief is that it originated in Anglo-Saxon times as a payment for the right to drive cattle over land belonging to the ancestors of the Duke of Buccleuch.

Cattle and Paganism

Cattle, especially bulls, have always played a part in pre-Christian worship. The bulls stipulated as a fine in the Wroth ceremony were domesticated by the Celts and came to be known as faerie cattle. The breed has died out with the exception of the one herd kept within the walled park of Chillingham Castle in Northumberland.

In Scotland, it used to be common for cows' milk to be poured into Dobby Stones, known as Leac an Grugach *in Gaillic, as an offering to the goddess Gruac, the protector of cattle.*

As Dawn Breaks

However it began, it is crucial that the ceremony commences just as soon as it is light enough to read the Charter of Assembly and that representatives of villages of the Knightlow Hundred (which now comprises parts of modern-day Coventry and Warwickshire, but was once all owned by the Buccleuch family) pay a consideration to the Duke. When their parish is called by the Duke's agent, they throw their dues – now the equivalent of 46p – into the hollow in the stone.

In days gone by, those who did not cough-up (1893 was the last time someone didn't) faced either a fine based on a pound for every penny owed or had to produce a white bull with a red nose and ears as payment.

After the ceremony is over, the payees head for The Dun Cow inn at Stretton-on-Dunsmore where toasts of rum and milk are made to the Duke of Buccleuch and a substantial breakfast is provided.

Halishy Nice Weather

The date of the Wroth Silver Ceremony is also St Martin's Day (see page 187). It often coincides with a brief, sunny mild spell and gave rise to the term, 'Halcyon Days'. An Alcyon (the 'H' was added in more modern times due to the fact that 'Hals' is the Greek word for sea) was a kingfisher-like bird in Greek mythology, and the phrase comes from the belief that a Halcyon could make the waters calm and tranquil in order to brood a late nest of hatching chicks before the winter weather set in.

Horseman's Word Ceremony

Although clothed in secrecy and despite denials as to its survival in the modern world, there is still a possibility that, like the Masonic lodges, the Society of the Horseman's Word still exists. Assuming that it does, it is safe to say that it is a custom from which ordinary members of the public are excluded. Nevertheless, it has such an interesting history that it is worth including here.

Everyone in Their Place

Victorian domestic staff and farm workers had a very strict hierarchy – a farm worker could, for example, marry a kitchen maid but would be frowned upon if he wished to marry the farmer's daughter. On the farm, unmarried workers often lived together in a room or 'bothy' and took their meals in a communal kitchen, and there was a definite procedure to be followed when either going in for a meal or heading out to work in the fields. The foreman – who was, in most cases, also first horseman – would lead, followed by the remainder of the staff in order of priority: the apprentice farm servant, known in some areas as the 'orra-loon', would be at the end of the queue. Having completed his apprenticeship, the orra-loon could, however, expect life to be a little less arduous once he had been initiated into the company of farm servants and given the Word, which symbolized harmony between man and beast (and, interestingly, power over women!).

And the Word Was

Huntly, in Aberdeenshire, was the centre of the Society of the Horseman's Word – a sort of Masonic group that comprised men who worked in trades connected with horses, such as farriers, blacksmiths and farm hands. New members were initiated upon reaching the age of 18 and normally inauguration would take place at Martinmas. Only an odd number of initiates could be confirmed at any one time – 13 being the preferred number. Invitation to the ceremony was the receipt from the society of a single horse's hair. Initiates had to take with them a loaf, a candle, a jar of jam or berries and a bottle of whisky.

The main point of the proceedings was to be told the Horseman's Word, which the recipients were told never to reveal to another living soul. As a test, immediately after being given the Word, they were asked whether they remembered what they had just been told. When they replied that they did, they were asked to repeat it. Anyone who then spoke it out loud, perhaps somewhat unfairly, failed the test. Finally, the initiates shook hands with the Devil, a man bizarrely dressed in skins, who held out a severed hoof: they were then expected to shake as if it were a human hand. The rest of the night was given over to celebrating.

Hush, Hush, Whisper Who Dares ...

The secret Horseman's Word was originally believed to be magic and guaranteed success in controlling any animals in the charge of its handler. It is nowadays considered more likely that the word passed between carters, coachmen and the like was nothing more than a secret 'recipe' – a series of instructions as to the best aromatic oils, which were known to calm animals down and make them more responsive. Herbs such as rosemary would be rubbed into the horse's forehead and added to their feed.

ARMISTICE DAY AND MARTINMAS (11 NOVEMBER)

Long before 11 November became known as the day on which the treaty signalling the end of World War I was signed, the date played a significant part in the history and customs of Britain. In pre-Christian times it was associated with Samhain and the Celtic New Year and in the 7th century it was adopted by the Church as Martinmas, the feast day of St Martin of Tours.

COUNTRY PRACTICES

For many generations, Martinmas was one of the days on which rents were due and land tenancies were either begun or revoked. Farm workers seeking employment at one of the many hiring fairs held around the country (see page 162) would refer to the day as Pack Rag Day, as it was quite often the date when they moved on to new employment. Scotland still treats it as one of their 'term days' and in times gone by Scottish farm staff who were moving on, quite literally to 'pastures new,' would organize a meal known as the Martinmas Foy for the colleagues they were leaving behind. The in-comers would then be given a similar party a few days later, this time hosted and organized by the existing workers.

St Martin and Wine

St Martin of Tours was a Roman foot soldier who went on to become a monk. He is best known for giving his cloak to a starving beggar one cold snowy night, and this has given rise to the expression St Martin's Summer, meaning an unseasonably mild spell of weather in winter.

Martin is also the patron saint of wine growers and the anniversary of his death on 11 November was, at one time, celebrated by French viticulturalistes with the release of the year's Beaujolais Nouveau wines. Eventually the date would coincide with Armistice Day and, as a mark of respect to the fallen, the launch of the new Beaujolais was moved to 15 November (it was subsequently moved again to the third Thursday of the month – probably to fashion a long weekend of the celebrations so beloved by the French!).

If it hadn't been done at Michaelmas, any surplus livestock would be killed and smoked or salted around this time to provide winter meat for the farming folk, but in certain parts of the country there was also a symbolic meaning to the killing of cattle, pigs or sheep. In areas of Scotland and Ireland, for example, if animal blood had not been ceremonially spilt on to the farmland, the following year would not be a fertile one. Parts of Ireland went a stage further and, according to R H Buchanan writing in *Ulster Folklife* (Volume 9; 1963), an animal was slaughtered on Martinmas Eve by the man of the house if it were a sheep or pig or by the wife if it was a bird from the chicken run:

"Its blood was then sprinkled over the house inside and out and over the byre and all the outbuildings. The sign of the cross was made in blood on both sides of the threshold and also upon the foreheads of all the children and other members of the family. If a fowl had been killed, its head was sometimes thrown over the house roof as a protection against evil in the coming year. When all this had been done, the slaughtered creature was eaten."

ARMISTICE DAY

After World War I, Armistice Day commemorated the end of the war on 11 November 1918. In 1945, at the end of World War II, this became Remembrance Day (or Remembrance Sunday), to include both wars, and was fixed to the nearest Sunday to 11 November. The day is still commemorated by local church services and a parade of royalty, politicians and ex-service personnel in London's Whitehall, during which wreaths of poppies are left at the Cenotaph. By tradition, at 11am, a two-minute silence is observed nationwide in honour of those who lost their lives.

Red Poppies

The poppy is traditionally worn on Remembrance Day in memory of members of the armed forces who lost their lives in World Wars I and II and subsequently in conflicts such as the Falklands War and the Gulf War. The red poppies represent the poppies that grew in the cornfields of Flanders in World War I where many thousands of soldiers lost their lives.

Firing the Fenny Poppers

Fenny Stratford, Buckinghamshire (11 November)

The Fenny Poppers are six curiously shaped miniature cannons, which are fired at 8am, noon, 2pm and finally at 6pm every 11 November. The tradition has been in existence for nearly 250 years and is a way of commemorating Dr Browne Willis, who was largely responsible for the building of the present church in Fenny Stratford in 1730: prior to that date the village had no place of worship at all. Dr Willis hit upon the bright idea of selling ceiling space in the new building, so that any local families prepared to donate £10 or more could have their coat of arms displayed: the success of this proved that one should never underestimate the power of advertising or vanity!

The original guns were re-cast in 1859, after one of them burst. They are nowadays regularly x-rayed to ensure that there are no cracks unnoticeable to the naked eye. Each one weighs 8.5 kilos (19lbs) and takes up to a quarter pound of gunpowder.

The ceremony has been held at several local sites, including the Canal Wharf, the churchyard, land behind the church, St Martin's Hall and finally, the Leon Recreation Ground, which is more auspicious than it might sound, as it was once part of land belonging to the Chantry.

A Right Load of Martins

Browne Willis had his church dedicated to St Martin in memory of his grandfather, who lived at St Martin's Lane, in St Martin-in-the-Fields and died on St Martin's Day, 1675. It would be good to say that his Christian name was Martin, but it wasn't … !

The Biggest Liar in the World Competition

Santon Bridge, Cumbria (third weekend in November)

Copeland Borough Council and Jennings Brewery are the joint organizers of The Biggest Liar in the World Competition, held annually at The Bridge Inn each November. You might assume from this that the event has been created as a publicity stunt to increase tourism and the consumption of local ale, but you would be wrong – this prestigious title originates as a result of the exploits and story-telling abilities of one Will Ritson.

Stretching the Truth

Born in 1808, Ritson was a farmer before becoming the owner of The Huntsman's Inn at the head of the Wasdale Valley. Despite his story-telling, he claimed never to tell lies, merely exaggerate the truth. One of the most famous of his stories was how he apparently managed to cross a foxhound with a golden eagle in order to produce a dog that could leap over the tallest of local drystone walls. Not all of his stories were original, however, and he adapted some local folklore to suit his own ends. The remote, beautiful valley was already well known for having England's deepest lake (Was-water), the highest mountain (Scarfell Pike), the small-est church (Wasdale Head Church) and all featured in his far-fetched bar-room chat.

Entrants attempting to win The Biggest Liar in the World Competition are allowed a minimum of

> *Tall Stories*
> *Previous winners' audacious mend-acities include a geological account of the formation of the Lake District through the action of giant moles, and a story about the fish-farming of mermaids. One winner apparently went on quite an action-packed holiday with the Pope.*

two minutes and a maximum of five to demonstrate their ability to 'lie'. The use of Cumbrian dialect is permitted, although 'props' are not allowed and overseas competitors have to provide their own interpreters if necessary. Interestingly, politicians, clergy and members of the legal profession have been barred from entry since the competition's inception.

The winner of the competition may be 'publicly billed, advertised or referred to as The Biggest Liar in the World for as long as he or she holds the title'. Entry is free – forms are available from the Whitehaven Civic Hall – and if you don't win, you can always console yourself with a helping of the traditional local stew, claimed by the event organizers to be made from a haunch of tiger beef!

Blessing the Silkies

Derriskellings, Ireland (first new moon in November)

In Derriskellings, a small fishing village in Southwest Ireland, the villagers gather each year to Bless the Silkies – magical folk who exist as seals in the sea but appear on the land in human form.

Centuries ago the village was at the point of starvation due to a long period of fruitless fishing. One night Maighdlin MacCail, a young girl from the village, told her mother that she had a dream explaining that if she was to go out to sea on a new moon and become a Silkie, the curse would be lifted. Despite her mother's tear-filled protestations, the young girl swam from the cove at the base of the village. She was never seen again in human form, but from that night great shoals of fish were caught every month on the same moon while a seal watched from the rocks.

The villagers gather on the shore and cast offerings of food and drink into the waves on the first new moon in November in order to bless the Silkies before spending an evening of thanksgiving at O'Holohan's Bar.

St Edmund's Bun

St Edmunds Day is 20 November. Edmund was King of East Anglia until captured by the rampaging Vikings, at which point things took a turn for the worse for him. Legend has it that on refusing to renounce his faith, he was put to death by a volley of arrows. His head was then cut off and thrown into the woods where it was taken away by a wolf. Later, as his supporters were searching for his remains, they heard a cry of 'here' and traced the voice to the wolf who, it appears had merely been protecting the severed head. On reuniting the head with its body the two are said to have miraculously fused together leaving only a faint red mark. Edmund was buried at – yes, seriously, he was – Bury St Edmunds.

In commemoration of this unfortunate Anglo-Saxon leader, the school children of nearby Southwold are each given a St Edmund's Bun after attending a short mid-afternoon church service on St Edmund's Day.

The Court Leet

Visit Wareham on any of the four evenings leading up to the last Friday in November and you'll enter a surreal world of Leather Sealers, Chimney Peepers, Constables, Ale Tasters, Carniters, Bread Weighers and Scavengers. Just after dark on any of these nights, a strange band of bizarrely clad men can be seen gathering outside one of the town's eight hostelries. Some are in hats, most are dressed in archaic clothing and all are wearing a medal suspended from a red ribbon.

Testing, Testing

Entering the pub the men use callipers to check the quality of leather goods, old scales to weigh a sample of the local bread and an ancient pewter measure to taste and report on the quality of the ale. Also present are the Surveyors and Searchers of Mantles and Chimneys (carrying old-fashioned sweeps brushes) whose job it is to check flues and fires. These men are the Officers and Jury of the Wareham Court Leet – a survival of an ancient local court that existed long before the days of local and central government. To this day, if they find fault with any of the products inspected they can levy fines for failing to maintain suitable standards – though the fines might be taken in the form of alcohol rather than money.

The court then sits formally on the Friday in the Council Chamber of the Town Hall at 12 noon (when the clock strikes 13) before adjourning to The Black Bear pub for a lunch paid for by the Lord of the Manor in gratitude for their services throughout the year.

NATIONAL FLOWERS OF BRITAIN

St Andrew's Day – patron saint of Scotland – is 30 November. The thistle was adopted as the Scottish national flower after an army of Norsemen landed at Largs during the night in the hope of surprising the sleeping Scottish clansmen. To ensure a stealthy approach, the Norsemen removed their footwear, but one inadvertently stood on a thistle and cried out, thus warning the Scottish troops of their arrival.

The flower of Wales is usually considered to be the daffodil, traditionally worn on St David's Day (1 March). However, the humble leek is also considered to be a Welsh emblem, possibly because its colours (white and green) echo the colours of the ancient standard.

In Northern Ireland, the shamrock, a three-leaved plant, was chosen as the national flower after it was said to have been used by St Patrick to illustrate the doctrine of the Holy Trinity.

The rose has been adopted as England's emblem since the time of the Wars of the Roses (1455–85) – civil wars between the royal house of Lancaster (whose emblem was a red rose) and the royal house of York (whose emblem was a white rose). The Yorkist regime ended with the defeat of King Richard III by the future Henry VII at Bosworth on 22 August 1485, and the two roses were united into the Tudor rose (a red rose with a white centre) by Henry VII when he married Elizabeth of York.

ATHOLL BROSE

The recipe of the traditional Scottish drink known as Atholl Brose was first recorded after an Atholl earl is reputed to have used the mixture to rid the Scottish king of a particularly troublesome Lord of the Isles in the 15th century. Another story has it that a young man in the area managed to rid the district of a wild savage by employing the intoxicating liquor and then claimed as his reward the hand in marriage of a young Atholl heiress. Make some if you dare!

    1 bottle of Scotch whisky
    10fl oz (300ml) of double cream
    1lb (450g) of honey
    Whites of 6 eggs
    1 handful of oatmeal

Soak the oatmeal in Scotch whisky. Beat the egg whites until stiff, then fold cream into them. Add the honey. Very slowly blend in the whisky and oatmeal. Pour into bottles and store for a week, shaking the bottles occasionally.

CHRISTMAS: ORIGINS AND CUSTOMS

Like many civilizations, particularly those located in the north where winter days are short and nights are long, the pagan Celts had celebrations around the time of the Winter Solstice (21 December), in part to brighten up the darkest midwinter days, in part to propitiate the gods to allow the sun to return.

The sun-god Attis was born on 25 December and the Romans worshipped Mithras at around the same time. Both were worshipped by the lighting of bonfires and it was believed that fire and flames would give the sun extra energy and encourage it to return. The lighting of brandy over the modern-day Christmas pudding is a relic of this. The Christian Church eventually took over the festival (and it is quite staggering to see just how close the story of the birth of Jesus corresponds with the birth of both Attis and Mithras – a child god born of an 'earth' virgin), but some of the religious traditions undoubtedly have pagan roots dating back to festivals held in honour of the heathen deities. During the Reformation, therefore, traditions such as burning the yule-tide log (symbolizing the light from the unconquered sun) were frowned upon by the Church. Amazingly, this state of affairs lasted in parts of the British Isles for nearly 400 years and it was not until the 19th century that some of the ancient Christmas customs and celebrations began again. Many of what we now consider to be established traditions – Christmas trees, decorations, presents, stockings at the end of the bed, carols and Christmas cards – originate from Victorian times and can be discounted in the search for ancient Christmas country customs.

YULE-TIDE

Yule-tide, now Christianized as the Christmas season, always began around 21 December – the longest night of the year – and included the New Year period. Some scholars believe the word is an adaptation of the word 'wheel,' indicating the turning of the year. In some parts of Scotland, Christmas Eve is sometimes still known as Sowan's Nicht, due to sowans (a porridge dish made from oat husks and fine meal steeped in water) being eaten. In addition, branches of the rowan tree were burned as a sign that any bad feelings between friends or relatives had been put aside for yule-tide.

The first Christian festival to be held on what we now accept as being Christ's birthday, 25 December, was supposedly celebrated by King Arthur in 521AD after he won the city of York; the date prior to this being dedicated to the gods worshipped by both the British Saxons and Danish invaders. The Roman festival of Saturnalia also terminated on this date.

ST NICHOLAS

And what of St Nicholas, without a visit from whom no child's Christmas would be complete? Again, it appears that the character of Father Christmas is an amalgam of pagan and Christian origins. As St Nicholas, he is the patron saint of children (among others), with a Saint's Day of 6 December and a propensity to dole out anonymous gifts of gold coins to those in need. In pre-Christian times he was thought to be the Saxon god Woden – a bearded, kindly looking man garlanded with ivy.

Ivy

Ivy, together with the leaves of bay and laurel, has always been used to decorate church windowsills and pulpits. Although laurel was used by the Romans as a symbol of victory – hence the laurel 'crowns' worn by Caesar and military generals – it was also used in ancient Rome as an emblem of peace and joy, long before its use was adopted by the Church as a way of showing that Christ had gained victory over the Power of Darkness.

Tin Can Band

At midnight on the first Sunday after 12 December the Tin Can Band plays and weaves its merry way through the streets of Broughton. But if you're expecting a beautiful rendition of the *Moonlight Sonata*, you are in for a huge disappointment as the whole point of this particular orchestral manoeuvre in the dark is to make as much noise as possible in order to frighten away the evil spirits of winter. Band members equip themselves with 'instruments' ranging from cans to pots and pans and metal dustbin lids. Nowadays, it is all quite good natured, but there have been times in the past when the occasion has got out of hand and riotous scenes ensued.

Making a din: Broughton's Tin Can Band

Tom Bawcock's Eve

Mousehole, Cornwall (23 December)

In Mousehole on 23 December the heroism of one Tom Bawcock is celebrated in a festival known as Tom Bawcock's Eve. According to local legend, foul winter weather had prevented the fishermen of the village from putting out to sea and the villagers' supplies of dried fish had long since been exhausted. Christmas feasting was likely to be nonexistent and so Tom, a widower, took his fishing boat from the harbour despite the dangerous conditions. Village folk could only watch as his little craft was buffeted by the storms and on several occasions – when it disappeared from view altogether – it was feared that it had capsized and Tom was drowned. But Tom survived and when he did eventually return to dry land it was found that he had managed to catch quantities of no less than seven different types of fish, which were used to feed the villagers and so save them from a miserable Christmas.

The story is re-enacted every year when a local fisherman sails into Mousehole harbour and unloads his catch from a small boat. Village schoolchildren carry fish-shaped lanterns in a musical procession around the narrow streets and hand out fish-shaped biscuits to other members of the community.

Village Lights

In remembrance of the tragic loss of life on the lifeboat Solomon Browne *during the Penlee disaster in 1981, the Christmas lights of Mousehole are turned off for an hour in the week before Christmas.*

Star-Gazey Pie

Traditionally eaten in Cornwall on Tom Bawcock's Eve (see opposite), star-gazey pie is unusual in that it has the heads of fish poking through the pastry. Originally the fish were cooked whole in the pie but nowadays they are cleaned and boned and their heads cut off. The fish (usually pilchards) are then laid in a deep dish and covered with milk and a thick pastry crust. The heads are pushed into slits cut into the pastry and the tails tucked under the edge before being baked in the oven. This local delicacy is usually served with a sauce of sour cream.

Elsewhere in Britain, what type of fish pie was eaten depended on where you lived – which is why there are so many regional variations and customs.

For centuries fish was considered to be a penitential food and it was not until the 15th century, when the Church decreed that certain days should be meat-free, that fish became to be considered a meal in its own right.

Medieval Britons would often mix fish and fruit. Mackerel and gooseberries were cooked in the same pie, as were cod and pears or crystallized lemon peel. In Yorkshire apples and potatoes were added to herring pies.

Tolling the Devil's Knell

Since the 13th century, the bell of Dewsbury parish church has been tolled every Christmas Eve (once for each year of the Christian era), supposedly to remind the Devil of his defeat when Jesus was born. Now with 2,000-plus years to toll, the business of the evening becomes more time consuming each year and nowadays it takes over two hours for the ringing to be complete. As can be imagined, the silence after the last bell tolls at midnight is somewhat eerie.

The custom has a secondary association with local landowner Sir Thomas de Soothill, who apparently murdered one of his servants and then donated a bell to Dewbury church in the hope of atoning for his heinous crime. The bell that rings the toll to midnight is named Black Tom after Soothill and the tradition is also known as Tolling the Old Lad's Passing Bell (so called because of the common practice of a bell being tolled on a death in the community).

Blessing the Crib

In common with many other churches, St Peter's Church at Hutton Cranswick begins its Christmas Eve celebrations with the Blessing of the Crib. Prior to this, tableaux are placed on the island of the village pond and in the vicinity of the church.

Because of their association with the stable at Bethlehem, farm animals are said to kneel in homage to Christ at the stroke of midnight on Christmas Eve, at which time they are momentarily blessed with the power of speech. Woe betides any human who overhears their conversation though – such eavesdropping is fatal!

Christmas Day Dip

Brighton, Sussex; Harve des Pas, Jersey; Bournemouth, Dorset; Polkerris, Cornwall; Porthcawl, Wales (25 December)

While to most people a Christmas Day dip conjures up nothing more alarming than an accompaniment to a cheesy snack and a gin and tonic before a turkey lunch, it takes on a totally different meaning around some parts of the British coastline. Here, intrepid, hardy and normally sensible members of the public choose Christmas Day morning to plunge into the sea.

Never warm at any time of the year, the British coastal waters in mid-winter are not for the faint-hearted. In Cornwall temperatures can drop below 50°F (10°C), while elsewhere, in the absence of the Gulf Stream, it can drop to a numbing 37°F (3°C) or less. Despite this, the practice attracts hundreds of spectators and dozens of participants to the above-mentioned beaches.

In Dorset, the Bournemouth Spartans take to the water from Boscombe Pier in fancy dress and you may well see Neptune, Vikings and octopuses emerging from the waves.

Serpentine Races

This winter madness is not confined to the coast though. Possibly the most famous Christmas Day Dip of all is organized by the Serpentine Swimming Club in London's Hyde Park. One of the oldest swimming clubs in the country, the SSC took the prospect of a 'dip' a stage further and introduced a competitive element: their first ever Christmas-tide race began in the late 1800s. In 1904 the novelist Sir James Barrie, author of Peter Pan, *presented the first Peter Pan Cup to the winner, replacing the gold medal formerly awarded. The race is open only to members and is raced on a handicap system.*

CHRISTMAS DAY SUPERSTITIONS

Do you hope for a sunny frosty morning in order to enjoy your Christmas pre-prandial perambulations? According to certain country superstitions you shouldn't!

Sunshine is fine in the afternoon (it foretells a good apple harvest) apparently, but if it appears in the morning the harvest fields will catch alight. Similarly, if it rains on Christmas morning you can expect a poor harvest, whereas a snowy morn will ensure that you have a good crop of hay.

The appearance of Jack Frost, known in pagan times as Jakul Frosti (Norse for icicle frost), must be treated with respect and a toast drunk in his honour. Heavy winds before nightfall is a portent of sickness and disease – whether that

is of crops or members of the household is unclear, but everyone knows the saying 'a green (mild) Christmas means a full churchyard' so you'd better not take any risks. If anyone in the family does die during the Christmas period, several other members of the family are likely to follow during the next 12 months.

Lucky Birthday

More cheerfully, however, those born on Christmas Day will be fortunate enough never to encounter a ghost, nor will they have anything to fear from spirits. They are also protected against death by drowning or hanging – making a lifetime career of piracy on the high seas seem an attractive choice.

Marshfield Paper Boys

Nothing at all to do with the delivery of your daily newspaper, on Boxing Day Marshfield's town crier leads a procession of characters dressed in paper costumes through the streets of the village. Beginning at the Market Place at about 11am and working their way down to a pitch outside the Elias Crispe almshouses, the paper boys perform the town's unique mumming play.

Why paper boys? Well, as already indicated elsewhere in the book, it was a fundamental necessity for the various performers such as guisers, Morris dancers and the like to preserve anonymity – for some, to be recognized broke the luck a particular activity was supposed to engender, while for others, to be identified could have repercussions from friends, family and employers.

The Rag Trade

Sometimes the disguise amounted to nothing more than a blackened face, but generally it consisted chiefly of strips of material fastened over ordinary clothes so that, in the better examples, almost the whole of the body was concealed in fringes giving a tiered appearance. A tall headdress may have formed part of the outfit, again covered with strips of material hanging down over the face so that the anonymity of the wearer was maintained. Once paper became readily available, strips of paper were often used in place of fabric.

So, get out your scissors and last week's colour supplements and get down to Marshfield.

BOXING DAY
(ST STEPHEN'S DAY)

The day after Christmas Day is more properly known as the Feast of St Stephen. St Stephen was the first Christian martyr to be acknowledged by the Catholic faith as a result of his being stoned to death in 35AD. Nowadays his saint's day has been somewhat hi-jacked by all manner of traditions.

In times past when the most important aspect of Christmas Day was its religious observance, presents, representing the giving of gifts to Jesus by the Three Wise Men, would be taken to family friends and relatives on Boxing Day. Historians say the holiday came about because servants were required to work on Christmas Day so took the following day off, and as they prepared to leave to visit their families, their employers would give them presents. Farmers' wives would make large pies, which they then sent around to the cottages of their husband's workers. It also became customary on this day for tradesmen to call on anyone to whom they had supplied goods during the previous year, in the hope of receiving a monetary gift, which would be placed in 'Christmas boxes'. As this retinue included lamp-lighters, errand boys, all manner of suppliers and journey-men, refuse collectors and quite literally, the butcher, the baker and the candlestick maker, it would appear to have been an expensive time for the well-to-do homeowner.

Traditions

Boxing Day traditions included a visit from hand-bell ringers in Norfolk; St Stephen's Breakfast in Oxfordshire; ale, bread and cheese in Buckinghamshire; and Morris dancing virtually everywhere. Despite the 2005 ban on fox-hunting, the traditional Boxing Day meet is still legal, provided the participants adhere to certain criteria, and is always well attended by spectators.

Hunting the Wren

Hunting the Wren, once popular throughout Britain, is still practised on the Isle of Man and in many parts of Ireland, particularly in the Munster counties of Cork, Kerry and Limerick. On Boxing Day groups of singers, musicians and dancers (almost always men or boys) known as Wren Boys dress in disguise and travel through their locality carrying an effigy of a dead wren (these days usually a small box symbolizing the wren's coffin, or a holly-bush on top of a pole symbolizing the tree or bush in which the wren is trapped and captured). A short, dramatic text telling of the death of the wren and promising good fortune in return for donations for a suitable burial and wake is sung or chanted.

Harsh Treatment

Boxing Day (*Gwyl San Steffan*) customs in Wales included that of the sadistic sounding holly-beating or holming, where it was customary for young men and boys to beat the naked arms of female servants with holly branches until they bled. In some regions it was the legs that took a beating, while in others it was the custom for the last person out of bed in the morning to be whipped with sprigs of holly and they would also have to attend to the needs of all the family for the rest of the day. A local explanation of this cruel tradition is that it commemorates St Stephen's barbaric death by stoning.

On many farms, horses and oxen were bled in a custom that was believed to be beneficial to their health, as it was supposed to increase their strength and to protect them from sickness throughout the year.

It would appear that Boxing Day was not a good time to be employed in service, late out of bed, a wren or a farmyard animal.

Mason's Walk

The feast of St John the Evangelist (27 December) is celebrated in Masonic circles across the world. Scottish freemasons have long held a particular affection for the apostle and in Melrose a torchlight parade around the market square has taken place every year on this date since 1745. The Lodge Brethren assemble after the annual general meeting and walk in procession following a route that goes up High Street, around the Market Cross three times, then continues through the town via Bow and Abbey Street to the abbey where a short ceremony is held within the grounds. On arrival, the procession is greeted at the gates by the ringing of the abbey bells.

Masonic Guilds existed in Scotland as early as 1057 and in England from around the early 13th century. They have always been connected with St John the Evangelist (also known as St John the Divine) and also associated with the Knights Templars – a powerful military order of warrior monks.

In the days when travel, education and communication were difficult, the various masonry guilds evolved a complicated and secret method of introduction to one another. This ensured that everyone was who they said they were and prevented fraudulent claims regarding suitable credentials for a particular job. There is a possibility that the connection between the Masons and Knights Templars arose due to the fact that the latter divulged some of their own particular rituals to their senior and more educated employees such as stone masons. Thank goodness for the advent of modern-day CVs and references!

HOLY INNOCENTS' DAY (28 DECEMBER)

Said to have originated in remembrance of King Herod's massacre of the first born son in his pursuit of the infant Jesus, Holy Innocents' Day, or Childermas, has always been deemed peculiarly unlucky. It was a day upon which no one, if he could possibly avoid it, should begin any piece of work. In Cornwall no housewife would scour or scrub on Childermas, and in Northamptonshire it was considered unlucky to begin any undertaking – or even to do the washing – throughout the year on the day of the week on which the feast fell. In Ireland it was called 'the cross day of the year' and it was said that anything begun at that time could not help but to have an unlucky ending.

As far as curious customs go, the day is remarkable for its association with whipping – not, apparently, in a sadistic way, but as a survival of a pre-Christian custom whereby whipping would expel harmful influences and drive out evil spirits. So that's all right then! Customs involving a similar ritual scourging could, at one time, be found throughout Europe: young men would whip the women and girls – if possible while they were still in bed; children would beat their parents and godparents with green fir-branches; while the menservants beat their masters with rosemary sticks, after which they would be given plum-loaf or gingerbread and brandy.

Mari Lwyd Mummers' Play

Of all the villages in Wales associated with the Mari Lwyd (meaning Grey Mare, although some believe that the name may have originally been Grey Mary) play, it is Llangynwyd that is chiefly responsible for maintaining the tradition – one of the strangest and oldest customs used to mark the passing of the dark days of a Welsh midwinter. As is the case with many pagan rituals to do with the cycle of death and rebirth, the Mari Lwyd involves an animal – in this case an uncontrollable 'horse'.

Traditionally, the horse and its attendants arrive at the door of the chosen house or pub and attempt to gain admittance with provocative challenges and insulting comments.

A Strange Entourage

The horse is made up of a real horse's skull, with false ears and eyes, which is attached to a pole carried by someone hidden beneath a white sheet. Reins, bells and ribbons complete the ensemble. The horse's jaw is often hinged and can be made to open and close from beneath the sheet. The attendants consist of five or six men and boys who wear coloured ribbons. Various other characters include the Leader, a Sergeant, a Corporal, Punch and Judy and a Merryman. The Leader holds the reins of the horse and carries a short wooden stick used to knock on the door.

Outwitted

Then comes a battle of wits (known as *pwnco*) between the people inside the door and the Mari party outside whereby challenges and insults in rhyme are exchanged. The battle, which lasts as long as the creativity of the two parties holds out, invariably ends with the horse and his crew winning the 'contest' and being allowed inside. There the horse chases and bites anyone in sight, while the Leader attempts, usually unsuccessfully, to restrain him. The other characters also each have a particular role to play: the Merryman is the musician of the party; Judy is traditionally supposed to sweep the hearth; and Punch careers around in an effort to kiss as many girls as possible before being turned upon by Judy who then attacks him with her broom. Despite the disruption and mayhem caused by the protagonists, it seems that the hosts are then expected provide both food and drink for everyone present.

Mari Lwyd Mummers in costume

Cleaning Up Their Act

The riotous behaviour of the Mari Lwyd gained such a bad reputation that chapel preachers advocated banning the practice, which was regarded as pagan and barbaric. In most areas of Wales the custom was eventually modified to include the singing of Christmas carols (often in English rather than Welsh) and the battle of insults was forgotten, but at Llangynwyd the original format seems set to continue. This old-style Mari Lwyd is also enjoying something of a revival among students at Aberystwyth University.

Mumming Plays

Mumming plays, known to have been performed for at least 1,000 years, have always symbolized the struggle between good and evil. Although there are many different characters, which may vary from play to play, the main point is usually to celebrate the legend of St George. Our hero faces up to a Turkish Knight or Infidel and a Dragon, with some of the other main characters being a Fool named Bedlamer, who carried a horn, and a man made up as Maid Marion. Cross-dressing seems a popular feature of many country customs and mumming was no exception.

The 'mummers' were masked thespians known as 'guisers' who originally performed at the spring equinox. In northern Europe at least this moved to the winter equinox when the changeover from the Julian to the Gregorian calendar (see page 11) was made and it became traditional for these plays to be carried out in December and January.

The best-known plays include a sword-dance, hero-combat play and wooing, and most have themes of death and rebirth which are jovially demonstrated before an audience.

A Motley Crew

The name and form of the characters can be traced back to the Crusades, but will vary from group to group. St George (and his Dragon) or the King (and his Steed) usually opposes the Turkish Knight. One is slain and miraculously cured by the Doctor with a magic cure-all-ills remedy. Minor characters include Old King Cole, Beelzebub and Johnny Jack, whose main job was to appear at the end of the performance asking for money – his costume was usually festooned with numerous rag dolls representing his many children and was a subtle reminder to the wealthy to be charitable at Christmas time. Topical characters were often added and have included notables such as Oliver Cromwell, St Nicholas, Napoleon and Nelson.

Guising

'Guising' comes from the old habit of dressing up in animal masks and costumes at the new year. It was frowned upon by the Church and in 690AD Archbishop Theodore wrote:

"If anyone, at the calends of January, goes about as a stag or a bull – that is making himself into a wild animal and putting on the heads of beasts – those who in such wise transform themselves into the appearance of a wild animal, penance for three years because it is devilish."

So there you are – the perfect get-out-clause when asked to perform in the annual village production!

Fire Festivals

Allendale, Northumberland; Comrie, Tayside, Scotland; Stonehaven, Grampian, Scotland (31 December)

The worship of fire is a practice that goes back thousands of years, and a number of fire ceremonies are still in existence all over the British Isles. Some take place on Twelfth Night to celebrate the midwinter solstice, but the three events described here have their celebrations six days earlier on New Year's Eve.

Allendale Fire Festival

Here a team of madly dressed Guisers throw blazing tar barrels filled with wood and wood shavings, known locally as 'kits', on to a bonfire and sing and dance until it is time to go first-footing (see page 12). Participating in the event is impossible for outsiders, as the Guisers are all local men.

Guisers carry flaming barrels at Allendale

Flambeaux Procession

At Comrie, you'll once again find men in strange costumes carrying huge torches around the village in a parade led by pipers, followed by a lively crowd of people, many of whom are also in fancy dress. The procession starts from the square on the last stroke of midnight, and there, after circuiting the village, it returns. The flambeaux (huge birch poles dressed with burning hessian sacking), still alight, are thrown in a pile on the ground and, around this makeshift bonfire, the crowds and torch-bearers dance together until it and they are all burned out. As at the Fire Festival of Allendale, participating in the Flambeaux Procession is a bit of a 'closed-shop', but is nevertheless, well worth watching from the sidelines.

Hogmanay

The origins of the word Hogmanay are uncertain. Some say that it is derived from the Norse Hoggunott *(night of slaughter) when animals were killed for a midwinter feast. Another suggestion is that it comes from 'Huh-me-naay' or 'kiss me now', reminiscent of a time when even complete strangers embraced. A third theory is that it came from a song called* Hogguinane *that was sung by French children.*

Fireball Whirling (aka Swinging the Fireballs)

At 11.30pm on 31 December the High Street of Stonehaven literally lights up as 60 local 'swingers' make their way towards the local harbour, all the time whirling perfectly spherical fireballs made of wood, paraffin-soaked cloth and wire mesh around their heads. Their arrival at the harbour is deliberately timed for the first stroke of midnight, when the blazing balls are thrown into the sea. The modern ceremony dates from a 19th-century fishermen's festival, but its true origins seem to stem from pagan times.

There are other theories on the significance of the festival, one of which relates to the Dark Ages and a bumper harvest that followed the sighting of a shooting star. Folklore has it that, attributing their good fortune to the sighting of the star; the villagers of Stonehaven introduced the annual ceremony in the hope of ensuring further fortuitous luck.

Fireball whirling at Stonehaven

Customs by Region

FESTIVALS WITH MORE THAN ONE LOCATION

The Silver Arrow Tournament 95
Various locations (second half of May)

Shrovetide Football 43-5
Alnwick, Northumberland; Ashbourne, Derbyshire; Jedburgh, Borders, Scotland (around Shrove Tuesday)

Christmas Day Dip 203
Brighton, Sussex; Harve des Pas, Jersey; Bournemouth, Dorset; Polkerris, Cornwall; Porthcawl, Wales (25 December)

Fire Festivals 214-16
Allendale, Northumberland; Comrie, Tayside, Scotland; Stonehaven, Grampian Scotland (31 December)

Cheese Rolling 85-7
The 'Randwick Wap', Stroud, Gloucestershire; Cooper's Hill, Brockworth, Gloucestershire; Stilton, Peterborough (Spring bank holiday)

SCOTLAND

Up-Helly-Aa 27-8
Lerwick, Shetland Islands (last Tuesday in January)

West Linton Whipman Play 102
West Linton, Peebleshire (first week in June)

Guid Nychburris 108
Dumfries, Dumfries & Galloway (third Saturday in June)

Braw Lads' Gathering 111-12
Galashiels, Selkirkshire (last week of June)

Herring Queen Festival 123
Eyemouth, Berwickshire (around second weekend in July, but dependant on tides)

The Burryman 136-7
South Queensferry, West Lothian (second Friday in August)

Braemar Gathering 151-2
Braemar, Grampian (first weekend in September)

Gathering St Michael's Carrots 161
Hebrides, (Sunday preceding 29 September)

Horseman's Word Ceremony 185-6
Huntly, Grampian (11 November)

Mason's Walk 208
Melrose, Borders (27 December)

THE NORTH COUNTRY

The Moot Horn Curfew 170-1
Ripon, North Yorkshire (every day of the year)

Goathland Plough Stot 20-1
Goathland, North Yorkshire (Saturday following 6 January)

Blessing the Salmon Nets 33
Norham-on-Tweed, Northumberland (14 February)

Scarborough Skipping Festival 41
Scarborough, North Yorkshire (Shrove Tuesday)

Kiplingcotes Derby 48-9
Market Weighton, Yorkshire (third Thursday in March)

Britannia Coconut Dancers 60
Bacup, Lancashire (Easter Saturday)

World Coal Carrying Championships 64-5
Wakefield, Yorkshire (Easter Monday)

Passing the Penny 67
Helpin, West Yorkshire (second Monday after Easter)

Planting the Penny Hedge 90-1
Whitby, North Yorkshire (Eve of Ascension Day,

40 days after Easter Sunday)

Midsummer Cushions 105
Bishops Auckland, Durham (21 June)

The Hepworth Feast 109
Hepworth, West Yorkshire (last Monday of June)

Warcop Rush-Bearing 115
Brough, Cumbria (29 June, but if this falls on a Sunday, 28 June)

Whalton Bale 118
Whalton, Northumberland (4 July)

Tynwald Ceremony 119-20
St Johns, Isle of Man (5 July)

Kilburn Feast 120
Kilburn, North Yorkshire (begins on the first Sunday after 7 July)

The Scarecrow Festival 138-9
Kettlewell, Yorkshire (a nine-day event usually running from the second Saturday in August to the following Sunday)

Rush-Cart Ceremony 142-3
Saddleworth, West Yorkshire (second weekend after 13 August)

Burning the Bartle 143-4
West Witton, North Yorkshire (Saturday nearest 24 August)

Egremont Crab Fair and Gurning Championships 156-7
Egremont, Cumbria (third Saturday in September)

Hop-Tu-Naa 178
Cregneash, Isle of Man (31 October)

The Biggest Liar in the World Competition 191-2
Santon Bridge, Cumbria (around the third weekend in November)

Blessing the Crib 202
Hutton Cranswick, East Yorkshire (24 December)

Tolling the Devil's Knell (aka Tolling The Old Lad's Passing Bell) 102
Dewsbury, West Yorkshire (24 December)

CENTRAL AND EASTERN ENGLAND

Haxey Hood Game 14-16
Haxey, Lincolnshire (6 January, unless the 6th falls on a Sunday, in which case it is held on the 5th)

Straw Bear Festival 18-19
Whittlesea, Cambridgeshire (weekend following 6 January)

Dwile Flonking 26
Kensworth, Bedfordshire (22 January)

Rocking Ceremony 31
Blidworth, Nottinghamshire (Sunday closest to Candlemas)

Hare Pie Scramble and Bottle Kicking 62-3
Hallaton, Leicestershire (Easter Monday)

Shakespeare Procession 74-5
Stratford-upon-Avon, Warwickshire (Saturday nearest 23 April)

Letting the White Bread Meadow 76-7
Bourne, Lincolnshire (some time in April)

Garland Day 100
Castleton, Derbyshire (29 May)

Love Feast 117
Alport Castles Farm, Derbyshire (first Sunday in July)

Dunmow Flitch Trial 121-2
Great Dunmow, Essex (every four years, around the second weekend in July)

Bonsall Hen Race 131-2
Bonsall, Derbyshire (first Saturday in August)

Abbots Bromley Horn Dance 153-5
Abbots Bromley, Staffordshire (first Monday after the first Sunday after 4

September. If the 4th is a Sunday, the event is held a week later on 12 September)

Old Man's Day 167
Braughing, Hertfordshire (2 October)

World Conker Championships 168-9
Aston, Northamptonshire (Second Sunday in October)

Wroth Silver Ceremony 183-4
Dunsmore Heath, Warwickshire (11 November, or the day before if 11th falls on a Sunday)

St Edmund's Bun 193
Southwold, Suffolk (20 November)

Tin Can Band 199
Broughton, Northamptonshire (first Sunday after 12 December)

WALES AND THE MARCHER LANDS

Dinas Bran Pilgrimage 61
Llangollen, Vale of Clwyd, Wales (Easter Sunday)

Knutsford Royal May Day 81
Knutsford, Cheshire (1 May)

Bawming the Thorn 107
Appleton Thorn, Cheshire (third Saturday in June)

The Wenlock Olympian Games 118
Much Wenlock, Shropshire (first week of July)

Mari Lwyd Mummers' Play 210-11
Llangynwyd, Wales (31 December)

SOUTH AND SOUTHEAST ENGLAND

Pancake Day Race 37-8
Olney, Buckinghamshire (Shrove Tuesday)

Swearing on the Horns 47
Highgate area of London (twice-yearly in March and July)

World Marbles Championships 58
Crawley, West Sussex (Good Friday)

Tichborne Dole 50-1
Tichborne, Hampshire (25 March)

Biddenden Dole 66
Biddenden, Kent (Easter Monday)

Tuttimen Hocktide Festival 69-71
Hungerford, Berkshire (second Monday after Easter)

Sweeps' Festival 84
Rochester, Kent (May Day weekend)

Gypsy Horse Fair 173
Stow-on-the-Wold, Gloucestershire (Thursdays nearest 12 May and 24 October)

Woolsack Race 96
Tetbury,
Gloucestershire
(Spring bank holiday
weekend)

**Searching for the Earl
of Rone 97**
Combe Martin,
Devon (Spring bank
holiday weekend)

Duck Feast 101
Charlton, Wiltshire
(1 June)

**Ebernoe Horn Fair
127**
Enernoe, West Sussex
(25 July)

Swan-Upping 128-9
Henley, Berkshire
(third week of July)

Hop Hoodening 158
Canterbury, Kent
(early September)

**British Lawn Mower
Racing Grand Prix
166**
Wisborough Green,
West Sussex (first
weekend in October)

**Lost in the Dark
Bells 167**
Twyford, Hampshire
(7 October)

**Titchfield Carnival
172**
Titchfield, Hampshire
(first weekend of
October half-term
holiday – third/fourth
week October)

Oyster Feast 173-4
Colchester, Essex
(last Friday in
October)

**Firing the Fenny
Poppers 190**
Fenny Stratford,
Buckinghamshire
(11 November)

**Marshfield Paper
Boys 205**
Marshfield,
Gloucestershire (26
December)

THE WEST
COUNTRY

**Wassailing the
Apple Tree 23-5**
Carhampton, Somerset
(17 January)

**Hurling the Silver
Ball 31-2**
St Ives, Cornwall
(first Monday after 3
February)

**Purbeck Marblers' &
Stonecutters' Day 42**
Corfe Castle, Dorset
(Shrove Tuesday)

**'Obby 'Oss
Ceremony 82-3**
Padstow, Cornwall
(1 May)

Furry Dance 88-9
Helston, Cornwall (8
May, except when that
falls on a Sunday or
Monday, in which case
the dance is held on
the previous Saturday)

**Nettle Eating Contest
103**
Marsham, Dorset
(around 18 June)

Golowan Festival 110
Penzance, Cornwall
(24 June)

**Marhamchurch
Revels 140**
Near Bude, Cornwall
(first Monday after 12
August)

**Crying the Neck
149-50**
Madron, Penzance,
Cornwall (first Friday
in September)

Widecombe Fair 159
Widecombe-in-the-
Moor, Devon (second
Tuesday in September)

**Tar Barrel Racing
179**
Ottery St Mary, Devon
(5 November)

**Turning the
Devil's Stone 180**
Shebbear, Devon
(5 November)

The Court Leet 194
Wareham, Dorset
(last week in
November)

**Tom Bawcock's Eve
200-1**
Mousehole, Cornwall
(23 December)

IRELAND

Sham Fight 124
Scarva, County Down,
Northern Ireland (13
July)

The Puck Fair 132-5
Killorglin, Co Kerry,
Ireland (10–12
August)

**Rose of Tralee
Festival 141**
Tralee, Co Kerry,
Ireland (a five-day
event usually running
from the third
Thursday in August
until the following
Monday)

**Blessing the Silkies
192**
Derriskellings, Ireland
(first new moon in
November)

PICTURE CREDITS

Acknowledgments

Much of the information necessary in the compilation of this book came about as a result of numerous telephone calls to various tourist boards, public houses in the relevant areas and local societies. Although I obviously introduced myself to them and explained the nature of my call, I did, on several occasions fail to note down the name of the person to whom I was speaking – either because the opportunity never arose or, quite simply, because I rather inefficiently forgot! My most grateful thanks and utmost apologies to you all.

Those whom I am able to thank by name include: Georgina Abbot, Michael Ayling, Margaret Clark-Monks (Burning the Bartle), Colin Cooper, Colin at the Kiplingcotes Derby, Mark Coyle (Hurling of the Silver Ball), Brian Glanfield (Burning the Bartle), Guy at Wasdale web design, John; the curator of the Carrot Museum (St Michael's Carrots), Liza Edwards, Stephen Friend, John Hadman (World Conker Championships), Fiona and Rupert Hitchcock, Jess Jephcott (Colchester Oyster Festival), Elisa Harrocks, William Kennings, David Nelson (Kettlewell Scarecrow Festival), Sarah Nicholson - Communications Officer for the Yorkshire Dales National Park Authority, the Revd Peter Norris, Michelle Parker, Phil Rant, the Hon. John Reeves-Morgan, Roger (Swan-upping), Tim Sandles (Crying the Neck), Andrew Skelton of Alport Farm (Love Feast), Anthony and Julia Smith, Canon Paul Townsend (Titchbourne Dole), Alan Turner, Brenda Wagstaff and Peter Wheeler.

Specific thanks must go to researcher Roger Morris, without whose assistance *Curious Country Customs* would even now still be at the planning stage. To my wife Melinda for her love, moral support and sorting out the computer when things went wrong. Permission to use previously published material is much appreciated and it is my great pleasure to acknowledge and credit the following sources (in no particular order):

Barbara Brown and the Earl of Rone Council (Hunting of the Earl of Rone)
Mark Constanduros: Press Officer for the British Lawn Mower Racing Association (BLMRA)
Coral Cornell and all connected with the Straw Bear Festival
Liz Flower and the committee of the Shakespeare Birthday Procession
Hop Tu Naa information is reprinted by kind permission of Manx National Heritage
Jean Kearney and Melia Communications – regarding happenings at the Puck Fair
Kerry Black and The Scotsman Publications (South Queensbury's 'Burryman' et al)
Gloucestershire County Council
Rex Needle: *A Portrait of Bourne* (available on CD-ROM), in connection with the Letting of the White Bread Meadow.

Pat Slaney and the Olney Town Council (The Olney Pancake Race)
Scarborough Borough Council (For permission to use website material appertaining to the Scarborough Skipping Festival)
Sarah Stevenson and others associated with the Tar Barrels (Ottery St. Mary) website
Stilton Parish Council (Stilton Cheese-rolling)
Stuart Walton and www.icons.org.uk (Morris Dancing)
Wendy Lough at Fantasy Prints (wendylough@fantasyprints.co.uk) (Herring Queen Festival)
Peter Thompson, Secretary to the Wenlock Olympian Society
Mr William Weston (The Braemar Gathering)
David Wheatley; host to the Wareham Court Let website
Wiltshire County Council

In addition, there are many other websites and links that have made it possible to verify facts, dates and the current state of various country customs. To all of these unknown contributors and compilers I am most grateful.

Dwile Flunking, although practiced at the Farmer's Boy, Kenworth for several years, had not recently been carried out at this venue and I like to think that it has been re-instated now as a result of my telephone conversation with the new owners. If that is the case, I have in my own way, been responsible for the continuation of a particular curious country custom and thank them for their help and enthusiasm in ensuring its survival. Brian and Shelia Ainley, owners of the Helpin Arms, West Yorkshire were also of great assistance with information regarding Passing the Penny – not only do they host the annual event, but they are also in charge of the fund-raising activities later in the year and were therefore in possession of all the necessary facts. Thanks too, to Susan Walshaw and the Gawthorpe Maypole committee for allowing me to use their website material concerning the World Coal Carrying Championships. The Society of Archers' kindly made available information appertaining to the Scorton Silver Arrow Tournament. I am also indebted to Father Keenan Haddigan, priest of Derriskellings, for his account of the Blessing the Silkic's ceremony.

Wherever possible, I have obtained permission to use material quoted; any omissions are only as a result of the trail going cold and will be rectified in any future editions if the original source is subsequently found.

Finally thanks to all at David & Charles who have been involved in this project; in particular Mic Cady, Louise Clark and Rebecca Snelling – as fantastic and friendly a team as any author is likely to experience. The jacket cover was designed by Sarah Clark and is, to my mind, perfect for a book of this nature – thank you so much.

Jeremy Hobson
Summer 2007

Index

Note: numbers in **bold** refer to photographs/illustrations. Numbers in *italics* refer to special features, including food features.

Abbots Bromley 153–5, **153**
Adrian II, Pope 182
agriculture 162–3, 187–8
Ainsworth, Harrison 122
alcohol 23, 25, 59, 66, 188, 196
ale 23
Allendale 214, **214**, 215
Alnwick 43–4
Alport Castles Farm 117
Andrew, St 195
Andromeda 73
Anglesey 55, 175
Anglo-Saxons 170, 183, 193
animal sacrifice 14, 188–9
aphrodisiacs 175
Appleby 173
apples 23–5, 35, 156, 177
Appleton Thorn 107
April Fool's Day *67*
archery 95
Armistice Day *187–9*
Arthur, King 198
Ascension Day 90–3
Ashbourne 42–3, 44
Aston 168–9
Atholl Brose *196*
Attis 197

Bacup 60
Ball Day 41
Ballycastle 133, 147
bank holidays 96–7, *145–6*
Bannock cakes 80
Barnet Horse Fair 164
Barrie, Sir James 203
Bartholomew, St 144
Bartle, Burning the 137, 143–4
Barwick 79
battle axes 152
Bawcock, Tom, Eve of 200–1
Bawming the Thorn 107, **107**
Beanjar *116*
Beating the Bounds *93–4*, 108
beatings 207
beauty contests 141
beer 66
bees 24

Beltane 80, 181, 182
Biddenden Dole 66
Biggest Liar in the World Competition, The 191–2
bikkos (straw dogs) 138
birds 25, 34, 207
Bishops Auckland 105
blacking-up 60
Blennerhassett, Harman 133, 134–5
Blessing the Crib 202
Blessing the Plough *22*
Blessing the Salmon Nets *33*, **33**
Blessing the Sea *92*
Blessing the Silkies 192
Blidworth 31
Boggan, Lord 14, 15–16
bonfires 176–7, 179, *181–2*, 197
Bonsall Hen Race 131–2
boot cleaning 36
Bosworth, battle of 195
Bottle Kicking 62–3, **63**
boundary disputes 93–4, 108
Bourne 76–7
Bournemouth Spartans 203
Bow-Wow Pie 126
Boxing Day 205, *206–7*
Boyne, battle of the 124
Braemar Gathering 151–2
Braughing 167
Braw Lad's Gathering 111–12
Bridget, St 46
Brighton 203
Brigid, St 30, 161
Britannia Coconut Dancers 60, **60**
British Lawn Mower Racing Grand Prix 166
Brough 115
Broughton 199
Browne Willis, Dr 190
Buccleuch, Duke of 183–4
Buchanan, R.H. 188
Bude 140
bull baiting 156
Burning the Bartle 137, 143–4
Burryman, The 136–7, **137**
Byrn, Lord 47

Caesar, Julius 11, 198
calendars
    Gregorian 11, 52, 212
    Julian 11, 212
Calennig 15
Candlemas *29–30*, 31, 52, 171
Canterbury 158
Canute, King 81

Carhampton 25
Caroline, Queen 101
carrots 161
Casanova 175
Castleton 100
Catholicism 113, 176, 206
cattle 24, 183
Celts 30, 41, 80, 104, 125, 147, 151–2, 176, 181, 183, 187, 197
Charles II 57
Charlton 101
Chaucer, Geoffrey 121
Cheese Rolling 85–7, **87**
chickens 131–2, 156
Christianity 9, 29–30, 32, 39–40, 53–4, 73, 88, 93, 98–9, 113, 176, 182, 197–8, 201, 206
Christmas 52, *197–8*, 200, 202–7, *204*
Christmas Day Dip 203
Christmas Eve 198, 202
Church Clipping *125–6*
cider 23, 25
Clay, Matthew 76
coal carrying 64–5, **65**, 166
Cobley, Tom 159
'Cock in Britches' 149–50
cock fighting 156
coffee houses 68
Colbran 183
Colchester 173–4
Combe Martin 97
Comrie 214, 215
conkers 166, 168–9, **168**
Cooper's Hill, Brockworth 85
Corfe Castle 42
corn dollies 149–50, **150**
Cornish wrestling 140
costumes 26, 37, 114, 155, 205, 213–15
Court Leet 194
cow cakes 24
Crawley 58
Cregneash 178
Crib, Blessing the 202
Crochon Crewys *36*
Cromwell, Oliver 133, 213
Cromwell, Thomas 98
Crying the Neck 149–50, **150**
cuckolds 127
Cumberland hounds 157
Cumberland wrestling 140
cure-alls 55

daffodils 195
dances 18–21, 60, 84, 88–9, 110, 113–14, 149–50, 153–5

David, St 195
Davis, William 167
de Dutton, Adam 107
de Soothill, Sir Thomas 202
debts 13
Deermen 153–5, **153**
Derriskellings 192
Derry, siege of 124
Devil 88, 160, 176, 180, 186, 202
Devorguilla 108
Dewsbury 202
Dickson, Isabel A. 136–7
Dinas Bran Pilgrimage 61
Dorset 94
dragons 72–3
drinks 23–5
    see also alcohol
Druids 176
Duck Feast 101
ducks 165
Dulse 147, *148*
'dumb' cake 178
Dumfries 108
Dunmow Flitch Trial 121–2
Dunsmore Heath 183–4
Dwile Flonking 26, 166

Easter 10, 53–66, *53–57*
Ebernoe Horn Fair 127
Edmund, St, Bun 193
education 68
Edward the Confessor 173
Edward the Elder 50
Edward the Martyr 42
eggs 53–5
Egremont Crab Fair 156–7
Elizabeth I 95, 128
Elizabeth of York 195
Eostre 53
Eyemouth Herring Queen Festival 123, **123**

Factory Act 146
fairs 127, 132–6, 147–8, 156–7, 159, *162–4*, 173, 187
Farmer's Walk 152
fasting 39–40
Father Christmas 198
Fawkes, Guy 180, 181
feasts 21, 32, 101, 109, 117, 120, 173–4
Fenny Stratford 190
Ferry Fair 136
fertility rites 14, 41, 53, 80, 84, 158
Filbelly *130*
fire festivals 10, 27, **28**, 80, 118, 176–7, 181, 214–16, **214**, **216**

Fireball Whirling 215–16, **216**
Firing the Fenny Poppers 190
First Footing 12
fish 201
Fishermen's Picnic 123
fishing 33, 123, 192, 200, 216
Fitzwalter, Reginald 121
Flambeaux Procession 215
Flodden Field, battle of 111
Flora 105
flowers, national *195*
Fools 14–15, **16**, 21, 97, 153, 154, 212
football 41, 42–5, **43**
using heads in 45
fox hunting 206
France 17
Freemasons 208
Furmitty *59*
Furry Dance 88–9, **89**

Gâche Cake *116*
Gaelic language 134
Galashiels 111–12
games 26, 31–2, 41–5, 58, 62–3, 179
Garland Day 100
Garrick, David 74
Gavin, Jim 166
Gawthorpe 64–5
George, St 72–3, 74, 82, 88, 212, 213
Glastonbury Thorn 107
Goathland Plough Stot 20–1, **20**
goats 133–5
goldfinches 34
Golowan Festival 110, **110**
Good Friday 58–9, *59*
goose fairs 163
gowks 67
'greasy poles' 156
Green Man 80, 82, 84, 100, *106*
Gregory XIII, Pope 11
Groaty Dick *130*
Groundhog Day 29
Gruac 183
Guernsey 116
Guid Nychburris 108
Guiseley Parish Church 126
guising 213, 214, **214**
Guizer's Jarl 27, 28
gurning 143, 157
Gypsy Horse Fair 173

Hal-an-Tow 88–9
Halcyon Days 184
Hallaton 62–3

Halley, Edmund 68
Halloween *176–7*, 181, 187
hand of friendship 164
Hardy, Thomas 59
Hare Pie Scramble 62–3, **62**
hares 53
harvests 147, 149–50, 162, 204, 216
Haxey Hood Game 14–16, **16**
heavy cake 149
Hebrides 161
Helpin 67
Helston 88–9
Hen Galen 11
Henley 128–9
Henry III 156
Henry IV 56
Henry VII 195
Henry VIII 98, 144
Hepworth Feast 109, **109**
Hereward the Wake 77
Herod, King 209
Highland Games 151–2
hippies 117
hiring fairs 162–3, 187
Hocktide 69–71, **69**, **71**
Hogmanay 215
Hole, Christina 158
holly 207
Holmes, Ken 49
Holy Innocents Day 209
Hood, Robin 81, 88
Hop Hoodening 158
Hop-Tu-Naa 178
hops 66
Horn Curfews 170–1
Horn Dances 153–5, **153**
Horn Fairs 127
Horns, Swearing on the 47
Horseman's Word Ceremony 185–6
horses 143, 186, 210–11
fairs 164, 173
racing 48–9, **49**
Hungerford 69–71
hunting 153–5, 206
Hunting of the Earl of Rone 97
Hunting the Wren 207
Huntly 185–6
Hurling the Silver Ball 31–2, **32**
Hutton Cranswick 202

Ia, St, Feast of 32
identity theft 51
Ireland 8–9, 11, 133–5, 141, 175–6, 188, 192, 207, 209
Irish language 134

Isle of Man 13, 119–20, 178, 207
ivy 198
Ivy Girl 150
Jack Frost 204
Jack O' Lanterns 176–7
Jack O' Lent 39
Jack O' Straw 138
James II of England 124
James IV of Scotland (James I of England) 112
James, St 127, 136, 173
Jedburgh 43, 45
Jesus 29, 40, 53, 56, 61, 107, 198, 202, 206, 209
John, St 208
John the Baptist, St 110
John of Gaunt 69, 113
Joseph of Arimathea 107

Kensworth 26
Kettlewell 138–9
Kilburn Feast 120
Killorglin 133–5
kilts 152
Kiplingcoates Derby 48–9, **49**
Kirna 150
Knights Templar 208
Knutsford 81

Lady Day *52*
'lambswool' 23
Lammas Day 52
Last Supper 56
lawn mower racing 166
Leafield 55
leeks 195
Lent 37, *39–40*, 54
Lerwick 27–8
Letting the White Bread Meadow *76–7*
Lewes 182
Licky Pies *78*
livestock markets 133–5, 159
Llangollen 61
Llangynwyd 210–11
London 47
long-sword dance 20–1
Lost in the Dark Bells 167
Love Feast 117
love tokens 34
Lowe, Revd. 155
Lugh 147
lying 191–2

Mabella, Lady 50
MacCail, Maighdlin 192
Madron 149–50
Magdalene College 80
Maiden 150

Malcolm III 151
marbles 58
Marching Season 124
Marhamchurch Revels 140
Mari Lwyd Mummer's Play 210–11, **211**
Market Weighton 48–9
marriage 46, 104, 178
Marsden, John 68
Marsham 103
Marshfield Paper Boys 205
Martin, St 184, 187, 188, 190
Martinmas 52, 186, *187–9*
Mary I 182
Mary the Virgin 29, 52
Mason's Walk 208
Maundy Thursday *56–7*
May Day 10, 79–84
maypoles 79
Melrose 208
Michael, St 73, 88, 160
Gathering the Carrots of 161
Michaelmas 52, 70, 162, 163
Midsummer Cushions 105
Mitchell, Hannah 117
Mithras 73, 197
Molly dancers 18, 19
moon 165
Moot Horn Curfew 170–1
Morris Dancing 84, *113–14*, 143, 169
Morwenna, Saint 140
Mothering Sunday 40
mountains 61
Mousehole 200
Mowbray, Lady 14
Mowbray Stone 15
Mulchinock, William Pembroke 141
Mummers 114, 143, 171
mumming plays 88–9, 210–11, *212–13*

nature worship 137
Nettle Eating Contest 103, 166
New Year *11–13*, 67, 187, 198, 214
Nicholas, St 198, 213
Norham-on-Tweed 33
Normans 153
Northern Ireland 124, 145–6, 147, 195

oaths 47
'Obby 'Oss 82–3, **83**
O'Connell, Daniel 134–5
O'Connor, Mary 141
Old Man's Day 167

Olney 37–8, **38**
O'Neill, Hugh, Earl of
  Tyrone 97
Oswald, St 126
Ottery St Mary 179, 181
Oul' Lammas Fair 133,
  147, 148
Oyster Feast 173–4

pace-eggs 54
Padstow 82–3
pagans 9, 14, 29, 41, 53–4,
  60, 62, 80, 88, 98, 147,
  158, 160, 176, 182–3,
  197–8, 204, 210–11, 216
Painswick 126
Palm Sunday 55
Pancake Day Races 37–8, **38**
Parade of the Apple Cart 156
Parsley Pies *78*
Passing the Penny 67
Patrick, St 46, 195
Pearce, Tom 159
Penlee disaster 200
Penny-Brookes, William 118
Pentecost 52
Penzance 110
Perseus 73
Philip, St 173
pies *78*, 126, 201
Pirate Dances 60
plague 57, 99, 109
Planting the Penny Hedge
  90–1, **91**
plays, mumming 88–9,
  210–13, *212–3*
Plough, Blessing the 22
Plough Monday 18–20
Plough Stot 20–1, **20**
Plough Sunday 22
poaching 153
poppies 189
proposals of marriage 46
Protestants 176
public holidays *145–6*
Puck Fair 132–5, **135**
pumpkins 126
Punch and Judy 210–11
Purbeck Marblers and
  Stonecutters 42
Puritans 79
purple 40

Queen of the May 79–80,
  81, 86

races 37–8, 48–9, **49**, 76–7,
  85–7, 96, 131–2, 157,
  166, 179, 181
Randwick Wap 85, 86
Reformation 197

reindeer 155
Remembrance Day 189
rents 70, 163, 187
Richard I 174
Richard III 195
Riding of the Marches
  94, 108
Ripon 170–1
Ritson, Will 191
robins 25, 34
Rochester 84
Rocking Ceremony 31
Rogation Day *93*
Roman Catholics 113
Romans 11, 66, 93, 140, 174,
  197–8
Rose of Tralee Festival 141,
  166
roses 195
Roundheads 134
Rush-Cart Ceremony 142–3,
  142
rushes 115

Saddleworth 142–3
St Ives 31–2
Salmon Nets, Blessing the
  33, **33**
sanding 81
Santon Bridge 191–2
Saxons 53, 94, 118, 198
Scarborough Skipping
  Festival 41
Scarecrow Festival 138–9,
  139, 166
Scarva 124
scolds 96
Scorton Silver Arrow
  Tournament 95
Scotland 8, 10–12, 46, 52,
  67, 80, 94, 108, 111–12,
  134, 136–7, 145–6,
  150–2, 161, 176–7, 183,
  185–8, 195–6, 198, 208,
  215–16
Scott, Sir Walter 112
Sea, Blessing the *92*
Serpentine Swimming
  Club 203
Shakespeare Procession 74–5
Sham Fight 124
shamrocks 195
Shebbear 180
Shrove Tuesday 36–37, **38**,
  39–40,
Silkies, Blessing the 192
Silver Arrow Tournament 95
Silver Ball, Hurling the
  31–2, **32**
Silver Ceremony, Wroth
  183–4

Simnel cake 40
skipping 41
Smoking the Fool 14
Somme, battle of the 124
Sonter's Day 111
South Queensferry 136–7
Southampton, 3rd Earl of 172
Southwold 193
sparrows 34
sports 41–5, 64–5, 118, 140,
  150–1, 156–7, 166, 168–9
Spring Equinox 212
spring-cleaning 40
Squab Pies *78*
squirrels 165
Star-Gazey Pie *201*
Stephen, St *206–7*
Stilton 85, 86–7
Stone Age 153
Stonehaven 214, 215–16
Stonehenge 104
Stow Gypsy Horse Fair 173
Stratford-upon-Avon 74–5
Straw Bear Festival 18–19, **19**
straw figures 138–9, **139**
Struan Micheil *160*
Summer Solstice 10, 52,
  104–5
Swan-Upping 128–9, **129**
Swearing on the Horns 47
Sweep's Festival 84

Tansey Cake 105
Tantalus 177
Tar Barrel Racing 179, 181
taxation 52
Tetbury 96
Thames river 128–9, **129**
Theodore, Archbishop 213
thistle 195
'Thorns' 107, **107**
Three Legs of Man 119
Tichborne Dole 50–1
Times, The 180
Tin Can Band 199, **199**
Titchfield Carnival 172
toffee 147, 148
Tolling the Devil's Knell 202
Tossing the Caber 151–2
Tralee 141
'transvestites' 153, 154
Tudor, Margaret 112
Tudor rose 195
Turning the Devil's Stone 180
Tuttimen Hocktide Festival
  69–71, **69**, **71**
Twelfth Night cake *17*
Twyford 167
Tynwald Ceremony 119–20,
  120

Up-Helly-Aa 10, 27–8

Valentine's Day *34–5*
Victoria, Queen 151
Vikings 14, 27–8, **28**, 119,
  193
Vine, Josiah 121

Wakemen 170–1
Walburga, Saint 182
Wales 8–9, 11, 13, 61, 94,
  195, 207, 210–11
Wall, Matthew 167
Warcop Rush Bearing 115
Wareham 194
Wars of the Roses 195
Wassailing *23–4*, 25
weather forecasting 61, *165*
Well Dressing *98–9*
Wenlock Olympian Games
  118
West Linton Whipman
  Play 102
West Witton 143–4
Whalton Bale 118
whipping 209
Whitby 90–1
Whittlesea 18–19
Widecombe Fair 159
Wilfred, St 171
William I 77
William III 124
Williams, Alex 103
wine 188
Winter Equinox 212
Winter Solstice 197, 198
Wirksworth 126
Wisborough Green 166
witches 53, 96
Woden 198
women's rights 117
Woolsack Race 96
working week 146
World Coal Carrying
  Championships 64–5,
  65, 166
World Conker Championship
  166, 168–9, **168**
World Marbles
  Championships 58
World Wars 187, 188–9
wrens 207
wrestling 140
Wroth Silver Ceremony
  183–4

Yellowman 147, *148*
Yule-Tide 197, 198